WALKS
on the
MENDIP HILLS

Cover: Crook Peak from Wavering Down

Overleaf: Map showing whereabouts of the 18 walks in this book

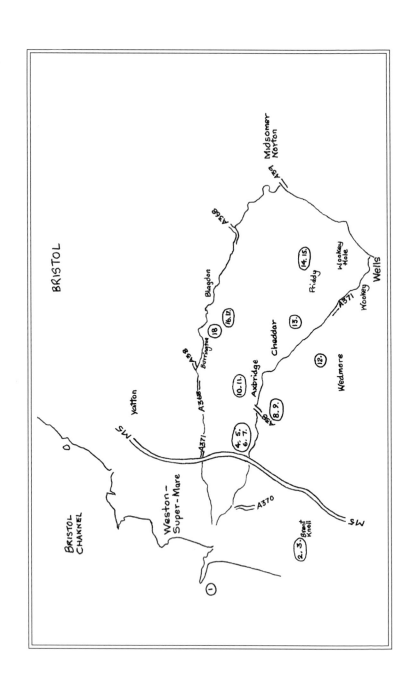

WALKS
on the
MENDIP HILLS

James Alsop

EX LIBRIS PRESS

Published in 2010 by
Ex Libris Press
11 Regents Place
Bradford on Avon
Wiltshire   BA15 1ED

Origination by Ex Libris Press

Printed by Cromwell Press Group
Trowbridge, Wiltshire

ISBN 978-1-906641-20-7

Dedication

To my friends and colleagues at Wiltshire College,
who during the past five years, have patiently
endured an eccentric in their midst.

CONTENTS

Introduction

THE WALKS

Introduction

The Mendip Hills (often referred to simply as the Mendips) constitute a compact and dramatic upland area quite unlike anywhere else in southern England, especially east of the M5. Rising abruptly from the remarkably flat Somerset Levels, their modest height illustrates to perfection that lofty altitude is not necessary to make an impression on the casual observer or serious explorer. Never exceeding 325 metres (m) (1066 feet (ft)) above sea level, and arguably at their most striking in the far west, where an average altitude of 200m (660ft) is typical, they nevertheless portray upland characteristics that even some devoted mountaineers admire. Somerset boasts no mountains but these hills sit proudly at the juxtaposition between the two and at the very least qualify for 'mountain-in-miniature' status. The following brief discussion attempts to provide a selection of reasons why this is so, before a more holistic appraisal of the Mendips' appeal is offered.

First, as already mentioned, these hills rise dramatically from a flat landscape so that every metre of height gain from valley to hill-top is significant, and leads inevitably to long distance views of unforgettable quality. Second, the range's southern slopes between the M5 and Cheddar in particular (but sometimes beyond, towards Wells too), are typically uncultivated and possess a rugged character, more in keeping with British mountains than lowland hills. Third, bare rock (Carboniferous Mountain Limestone) protrudes at regular intervals, providing an aesthetic quality and underfoot sensation, with which many a mountain connoisseur will be immediately familiar. Fourth, in the small area between Loxton and Shute Shelve Hill, a selection of quite narrow ridges provide ascents onto the Mendip plateau, adding yet another dimension to the upland appeal of the range. Fifth, the region is blessed with a number of spectacular gorges, most notably at Cheddar (see page 15) and Burrington (see page 85). The former is dominated by sheer rock towers that seem strangely out of place in gentle south-west England, whilst the latter, though slightly less awe-inspiring, boasts jaw dropping vistas, from both the top and bottom of steep-sided, rocky slopes. Sixth, the exposed nature of the hills and their westerly location ensures that the climate, though moderate, is breezy and sometimes subject to rapid change, when sea mists roll in or an Atlantic depression intensifies as it rises to pass over the Mendip plateau.

Combining these and other aspects, the Mendips, though modest in scope and height, provide a delightful upland diversion, combined with an improbable intimacy that renders them unique in southern England.

The Mendips are the most southerly range of Carboniferous Limestone hills in England. Their closest relative is the Peak District in Derbyshire (the UK's most visited national park). Both regions share typical limestone characteristics including dry valleys, dramatic cliffs and gorges, wooded areas, sweeping plateaux that are ideal for grazing, and dry stone walls. If approaching the Mendips from the north this latter aspect provides more than a hint that a distinctly different region has been entered into, even though the steep southern slopes are hidden and long range views obscured.

Another aspect of the area's appeal is the striking diversity contained within such a small area. The highest portion of land, Beacon Batch, is little more than a gentle upland plateau of Old Red Sandstone, markedly different from the hills' southern aspect, and yet these contrasting landscapes can be easily linked during walks of modest length and manageable terrain.

Neither should one fail to note how the various settlements of the Mendips add to the region's allure. Picturesque villages are liberally scattered throughout the area, beneath the hills to the south, across the plateau and beyond the northern slopes too. Naming them all at this point would be impractical, but where appropriate many are mentioned with the descriptions of the walks.

The Mendips are a sensitive area both scenically and ecologically, but are well protected by both statutory and voluntary bodies. 80 square miles (200 square kilometres) of the range, between Bleadon in the west, Chew Valley Lake in the north-east and Wells in the south-east (a neat, logical and easily definable area), fall within the Mendip Hills Area of Outstanding Natural Beauty (AONB). AONBs have a statutory duty to protect and preserve scenically significant areas in much the same way as national parks, but are administered locally, and don't place as much emphasis on the promotion of access as the latter.

Separately, the National Trust, one of Europe's largest conservation charities, owns and manages 27 square miles of the Mendips, including some of the most celebrated sites and viewpoints (Crook Peak, Wavering Down and parts of Cheddar Gorge to name a few), ensuring access remains open and comprehensive on an ongoing basis.

Scope of the Mendips

Defining the scope and boundary of the Mendips is a relatively straightforward exercise. Their small scale helps in this respect but pouring over relevant maps (OS Landranger 182 and OS Travel Map South-West England especially) also aids one to quickly comprehend and appreciate Mendip geography.

From west to east, the true mainland boundary of the region is glorious Brean Down, the prominent limestone headland that pokes out into the Bristol Channel but is cut off from the main plateau by the river Axe, which flows into the sea from its source in Wookey Hole, just west of Wells. The eastern extremity is Egford Hill on the outskirts of Frome. In the south the region is perhaps most easily defined, where the hills rise abruptly from the extensive Somerset Levels (often referred to as The Levels – throughout the guidebook I have used both terms interchangeably); the A371 running between Shepton Mallet and Axbridge also helps to enclose the area, albeit artificially. The northern terminus is not quite so sharply defined but steep slopes (between Blagdon and West Harptree) as well as the A368 and B3114 help to complete the Mendip boundary, though the north-eastern fringes are more vague and difficult to delineate, both on the ground and when studying the map.

As the crow flies, from west to east, the Mendips are approximately 30 miles across, but from north to south, even at their widest, they do not extend over more than a 7 mile area. This easily manageable range is therefore ideal for those who love to become familiar with an area, without the need for constant motorised assistance.

Scope of this guidebook

The scope of this guidebook is smaller than the Mendip region but this is quite deliberate on my part. The walks are initially laid out from west to east, beginning on Brean Down, and displaying an obvious bias towards the more dramatic south-facing slopes and hill-tops. The outliers of Brent Knoll and Nyland Hill are included because of the magnificent opportunities they provide to appraise the range from nearby vantage points. In the east I have not included any walks beyond Wells, as beyond this splendid little city (the smallest in England), the hills melt somewhat, while the Levels lose their uniform flatness, thus definitions are considerably blurred. To the north three walks are described (this time, east to west) but circular ones across the plateau only, are not, because the drama of the hills is not so apparent, despite the appeal to some, of such alternative landscapes and gentler terrain.

Hill-top summits

Despite their upland qualities the Mendip Hills are not famed for conspicuous and individual summits, rather the high ground, even where it tumbles steeply towards the Somerset Levels is typically homogeneous. Nevertheless there are some delightful exceptions to this rule, that add to the region's appeal and distinctiveness. What follows therefore is a west to east description of the most prominent hill-top summits, in terms of the views both of and from them.

▲ Brean Down 97m (318ft)

Though this hill is of modest height even by Mendip standards, it boasts a breathtaking panorama, affording views that extend to all points of the compass. To the west, sitting proudly in the Bristol Channel, Steep Holm, a limestone relative of the Mendips but cut off by three miles of sea, draws deserved attention, while beyond, a precise westerly bearing leads without further obstruction to the Atlantic Ocean. But still west, the narrowing of the Bristol Channel ensures that both the Exmoor and South Wales coastline can be admired. To the north-east the town of Weston-super-Mare fills the foreground, while east, the higher ground of the Mendips dominate. Then finally to the south, the Levels, Brent Knoll (isolated and very prominent) and the glorious sweep of Brean and Berrow Sands complete the 360 degree panorama. Even if a visitor had travelled many a mile to visit the Mendip region, this view alone would amply repay the effort and render the journey worthwhile.

Looking towards the summit of Brean Down

Brent Knoll from Brean Down

▲ Brent Knoll 137m (450ft)

Although this hill cannot quite match the aesthetic appeal of Crook Peak or Brean Down, the sensational view from its summit (a surprisingly large plateau in fact) is second to none in the region and beyond. The extraordinary panorama includes the Mendip chain from west to east, the Levels, the Quantocks and Exmoor, but most especially, the Bristol Channel, which from this vantage point is nothing less than the mighty Atlantic. Seeing these waters and the Berrow and Brean coastline for the first time from the summit, is mesmerising, emotional even! What is more, the summit plateau is so extensive, and the plateau edge so suitable for strolling, that several hours of quiet observation can slip by in a flash. Not even Crook Peak can match such an ideal summit observation point, even if its rocky edifice takes first prize for appearances.

Be sure to add copious amounts of time to any planned walk to this hill-top, thus ensuring summit views can be studied at length.

▲ Crook Peak 191m (626ft)

In almost every respect Crook Peak surpasses all other Mendip hill-tops. Sporting a true pointed summit of bare, rugged limestone, it is prominent for miles around. Further, it throws down a supreme ridge-cum-spur to the south-east which falls gracefully all the way to the valley floor. From many angles (west in particular) even without its rocky perch the hill would draw devoted admirers, but this feature adds considerably to its aesthetic appeal.

Neither do the views disappoint! Whether sitting or standing on the summit rocks, this view can be so overwhelming that it is appropriate to repeatedly rotate oneself, to absorb all aspects of the extensive panorama. To the north Clevedon can be picked out, while the eastern aspect is dominated by the Mendip range as it arcs around Cheddar Reservoir, before turning south-east towards Wells. When visibility is reasonable or better, to the south, south-east Glastonbury Tor can be clearly seen, while south in general, the Somerset Levels invite detailed study.

If the view ended at this point it would already be a splendid one, but some of the finest aspects are still to be enjoyed. To the west lie the Quantocks and Exmoor, the striking height of both being obvious from this vantage point: there is also a wonderful view out over the remainder of the range, to Brean Down and the Bristol Channel coast.

And, when clear conditions prevail, the remarkably prominent Foreland Point in North Devon, lying just east of Lynton and Lynmouth, is easily identified. If you've walked the South West Coast Path to the west of this exposed headland, in your mind's eye you will be able to soar like an eagle from Clevedon in the north to Morte Point in the extreme west, where North Devon meets the open Atlantic.

It is not possible to describe every feature of the view in a few lines of a small guidebook such as this, thus there is no alternative but to climb the hill for yourself, with time in hand to absorb the view in every direction – during the ascent, on the summit and when descending.

Crook Peak, Wavering Down and Cross Plain from Shute Shelve Hill

▲ Wavering Down 211m (692ft)

Occupying the highest ground in the Mendips west of the A38, this hill commands attention from the east and south, but is seen to best advantage during the ascent of Cross Plain. From this ridge it can be studied from summit to sea level, and its shapely form admired at leisure. Summits views are (unsurprisingly) superb, and include Crook

Peak from the east, the Bristol Channel coastline, Winscombe nestled in the valley, as well as much of the Mendips including a close up view of Shute Shelve Hill. Perhaps the only disappointment is the fact that the summit is set back from the edge of the hills and thus they do not drop away at one's feet.

▲ Shute Shelve Hill 233m (764ft)

It is not so easy to decipher the true summit of this hill, and strictly speaking it merges into a plateau shared with Axbridge Hill, Fry's Hill and Callow Hill. However, due to its National Trust ownership and uncultivated appearance, it does appear as a separate entity, and boasts a highest point immediately prior to the steep descent down into Axbridge village. Therefore, despite the lack of a trig point or other summit paraphernalia, it is a splendid viewpoint. The eye will be drawn both west (to Wavering Down, Crook Peak and the Bristol Channel) and south (to the Levels), but views east are excellent too, with Cheddar Reservoir being especially prominent.

Higher than any Mendip ground to the west, Shute Shelve Hill also possesses a discrete but discernable superiority over its lower neighbours, that appear subservient despite their own copious qualities.

▲ Nyland Hill 76m (249ft)

This splendid little hill is one of perfect shape and form. Despite its small area and modest height, it is conspicuous for miles around, being visible from all over the Levels, Brent Knoll, Brean Down even, and of course, the main Mendip chain. However, the view from the summit is arguably its most endearing characteristic for, from here, a superb opportunity exists to observe the Mendip Hills from Brean Down to Wells, with only a small cluster of summit trees partially obscuring the vast panorama.

▲ Beacon Batch 325m (1066ft)

Beacon Batch is an inconspicuous summit, representing little more than a swelling of the moorland plateau; nevertheless, the height supremacy it boasts over all other Mendip viewpoints, and the unique location and surroundings on offer, compared with summits further south, make it a splendid viewpoint.

▼ Cheddar Gorge

Cheddar Gorge is the most spectacular feature of the entire Mendip region (and arguably beyond) and thus it justly merits a section of its own at this point. Slicing through the Mendip plateau, it represents a quite uncommon geological phenomenon in Southern England. Scientists still guess at how it was formed, one theory being that the gorge was once a cave whose roof over time was compromised by the waters that formed the cave in the first place, leading to an extraordinary collapse and thence to the sheer-sided canyon in existence today. Whatever its origins, its modern day appeal is beyond question.

Approaching from the north, the landscape is intriguing enough as the top of the gorge is reached via the B3135, but as the descent continues, around each corner the scenery intensifies; bosky slopes give way to ever steepening rock, and when the narrow road is forced through a small, rocky gap, one is at the heart of the action. Even after disembarking and standing upright, necks have to be strained to appreciate the sheer-sided cliffs that climb almost 140 vertical metres (460 ft) into the sky.

Cheddar Gorge

From the south the gorge is much tamer to begin with and has been somewhat spoiled by intense development to take advantage and meet the needs of tourists. Perhaps this is a somewhat unkind observation, as locals do need to make a living and most tourists, especially those of a sedentary nature, are drawn to areas with good facilities and services. However, the development is hardly in keeping with the setting, and it seems incomprehensible that such a development could be repeated from scratch, in the heart of an AONB today. But shops, restaurants, cafés and ticket booths apart, the arrival in the heart of the gorge is still a thrilling experience that is unlikely to be forgotten.

To the west much of the immediately adjacent land is owned by the National Trust, thus access from the gorge bottom is feasible at certain points. However, slopes are steep, stony and often perilously close to much more dangerous terrain, therefore, only the experienced and cautious should attempt such a venture. Though it is a wonderful experience to drive into the gorge (better still walk), park the car and clamber high on one of the more manageable paths, to gaze with incredulity down into the canyon, for obvious safety reasons none of the walks start or finish in this area. But do not allow this as an excuse for you to avoid the gorge, for only after a long and ponderous appraisal of its grandeur can a holistic appreciation of the Mendips be acquired.

▼ The Bristol Channel

The sea is an ever present friend of the Mendip area featured in this book, it being clearly visible, in reasonable conditions or better, on all of the walks, and integral to the diverse appeal of most. Therefore to ignore a brief discussion of its character would be inappropriate.

Boasting the second greatest tidal range in the world and extensive mud flats between Sand Point and Burnham-on-Sea especially, some spurn its charm hereabouts, noting how it is often possible to spend a day at Weston-super-Mare, for example, without seeing the sea at all. This tidal feature also comes with considerable dangers for the unaware; the exposed mud flats can be treacherous, trapping victims who stray too far, and when combined with a rapid incoming tide, the life-threatening risks become all too apparent. The waters themselves are dangerous too, as the strength of the tide can be hard to swim against when out of one's depth.

But this is only part of the story, for the Channel has myriad charms that more than compensate for any negative aspects. The smell of sea salt and the sound of gulls tell the unmistakeable story that this is the sea and not just a large estuary. The water, though murky from river mud, is not dirty, meeting and often exceeding minimum EU bathing standards at the key resorts dotted along the coastline. When the tide is in, resorts like Weston enjoy shallow, warm waters, breaking onto golden sands – ideal for frolicking children (and adults!). Views across the Channel to South Wales are often stunning, and provide the opportunity to spot well known hills and other landmarks from entirely different angles. But, perhaps best of all, here is a stretch of coast that possesses pleasant and unexpected surprises. Take for example Brean Down from the south, when approached via Brean Sands. The juxtaposition of golden sand and dramatic rocky headland is more akin to the Gower Peninsula than the Bristol Channel. Sheltering under this rocky fortress is pleasant enough, but after climbing onto the Down, views south along the sandy coastline seem everlasting. At the western end of the Down, the ridge falls smoothly to meet the sea, and here the waters are never out of sight, or in the distance even. Thus the fear of not seeing the sea, prevalent in resorts immediately to the north and south, is irrelevant. For further comments on this serene location, see walk 1.

Another delightful surprise some way to the north is the quaint seaside town of Clevedon. This town, in my opinion, is unsurpassed until the finest resorts of North Devon are reached, and even then its charms compare favourably. With the largest tidal difference on the Bristol Channel (47 feet between low tide and high tide during springtime, when differences are at their greatest), potential visitors with no personal experience of the town, could be forgiven for assuming that one will see even less of the sea than at Weston and Burnham. However, the tidal difference is one of depth and not distance, thus in this priceless spot, the sea is always close at hand. Admittedly it recedes to reveal the mud flats so typical of the Bristol Channel, but when the tide is in, the sea laps onto the town's small pebble beach, affording excellent access to the water. Hours can be whiled away gazing across the Channel to South Wales, admiring the rocky bluff where the beach terminates, studying the Victorian pier (glorious in its simplicity), chatting to locals proud of their town and soaking up (even joining in with) the excitement when

Brean Down and Brean Down beach

Clevedon's bay, beach and pier

the swimmers' club meet for their high tide dip. Coupled with ample parking, a picturesque seafront with pastel-coloured houses and good views of the Mendips from the end of the pier, Clevedon's charms are beyond question.

If you are tired of this rather lengthy assessment of the Bristol Channel I apologise, but bear one more thought in mind; family commitments and circumstances often render it difficult to walk for a whole day, leaving keen walkers searching for a compromise. Combining a walk on the Mendips with fun on the beach is a delightful prospect. An awareness of tide times makes it possible to walk in the morning, arriving in the afternoon at one of the region's beaches; with high tide imminent and a summer swim planned, what better complement could there be to the earlier activities of the day?

▼ The Somerset Levels

In many respects, though opposite in terms of character and terrain, the Somerset Levels and Mendip Hills are inseparable. Some walkers (hill lovers especially) are inclined to dismiss the Levels as dull and uninteresting, but this is unfair and indeed ill-informed, as I hope to briefly illustrate below.

First, without the Levels, the Mendips' southern slopes would be a good deal less impressive on approach from the south. Driving north along the M5 and A38, or from a string of minor roads including the B3151 from Wedmore, the Mendips rise from the flat landscape appearing rather like a distant mountain range. Those who have made such a journey may well have shared the author's experience of a quickening pulse combined with eager anticipation as the hills draw near. Second, viewed from the southern edge of the Mendip plateau, the Levels represent an immense sweep of countryside. If the landscape was more undulating, long distant views would be much diminished, and the wonderful sense of space from east to west substantially curtailed. Third, the Levels are both attractive and important in their own right, offering not just an interesting alternative landscape through which to drive, but a place where the walker will be at home, enjoying mile upon mile of possible walking options. Fourth, these Levels are recognised internationally for their status as an environmentally sensitive area. Until the eighteenth century this was open marshland with occasional sandbanks, but drainage schemes were constructed that give us the unique landscape we enjoy today. Every aspect of life on the Levels including the farming industry, plant life, insect eco-systems and bird species are dependent on this carefully balanced management of water. If the drainage systems were too effective much of this fragile environment would change irreversibly but, if they were inadequate, the region would once again become a giant marsh. Fifth (and finally) the dramatic contrast between hill and plain that is so striking where the Levels meet the Mendips is indicative of the remarkable variety of landscapes to be found throughout Britain. Surely without these wonderful contrasts our little island would be a far less exciting and interesting place.

Cheddar Yeo

Weather on the Mendips

Visitors to the Mendip Hills seeking information about the climate, and in particular rainfall levels, could easily be misled into thinking the region shares similarities with much wetter parts of the UK. References to the rapid changeability and damp nature of the climate tend to create the impression that battling with the weather will be a considerable obstacle.

However, the truth about Mendip weather is far more promising and the vital statistics surprisingly benign.

The hills' westerly location and height above sea level, compared to surrounding lower lying areas, do result in slightly higher than average regional rainfall, but it's all relative. In reality, the Mendips experience remarkably moderate amounts of rain, in all seasons. Statistical sources vary slightly, but much of the range receives little more than 40 inches per annum. Compare this with the settlements of Fort William (in the Scottish Highlands and under the shadow of Ben Nevis – Britain's highest mountain), Ambleside (in the Lake District) and Princetown (on Dartmoor) all of which receive between 75 and 80 inches per annum. Further, the higher ground in the immediate vicinity of these areas receive very much more rain again (e.g. the summit of Ben Nevis receives more than twice as much as Fort William!) Yes, the weather is more changeable than adjacent, low lying areas, and the exposed nature of the hills does result in typically colder and stronger winds on the higher ground, but the well prepared have little to fear from the climate, unlike explorers of true British mountain areas, whose plans can be ruined and safety threatened by severe and volatile weather conditions.

When to walk

Providing you are well prepared, you can happily walk on the Mendips during all seasons. Spring and autumn are perhaps the best times for their contrasts of new life, vibrant colours, golden hues and cool breezes. But summer is marvellous too, as one feels the unbridled warmth of the sun and is able to contemplate that coastal afternoon dip referred to earlier. And winter throws up its own delights, with long, uninterrupted views, picturesque frosts and occasional snowfall.

One of the greatest benefits of upland aesthetics (rocky, exposed, steep-sided, uncultivated hills) in a lowland climate setting, is the year-round access available to reasonably fit walkers. With this thought in mind, enjoy these lovely hills in all seasons, and revel in the opportunity they provide to experience the Mendips' many and varied moods.

Equipment required

You will not need to invest a fortune equipping yourself to walk on these hills. Even in winter, adequate outdoor clothing, rather than the latest top-of-the-range wind and waterproof items, will more than suffice. However, it pays not to be too casual and to adhere to a few basic principles, both to ensure that a level of comfort can be assured, and to reduce the risk to health from exposure to cold winds and heavy rain.

Excepting stable, high pressure, sunny summer days, a light waterproof coat of reasonable quality or better, should be carried on all occasions. Rain and wind can be a miserable combination even if one is only temporarily caught out by a rogue shower. Further, once the body has been severely chilled, if wet it can be extremely difficult to dry out and warm up again.

In all seasons the secret is to wear light, man-made layers that wick away sweat, and can be easily removed or replaced. During winter a base layer will help during colder spells, especially if strong winds are a major contributor, and a warm hat and gloves should be considered essential items. In the summer months sunglasses and a cap will help reduce any negative effects associated with prolonged exposure to strong sunshine. Otherwise there is little to worry about. Erring on the side of caution is no bad thing, especially if you have spare capacity in your rucksack, but common sense should dictate such a course of action anyway.

Maps, rights of way and access

There is scarcely another country in the world more privileged than Britain when it comes to good quality walking maps. Both the OS Landranger and Explorer series are of such a high standard that there really is no excuse for heading into the hills without one. In addition, such maps enable walkers to plan their expedition in advance and to savour it afterwards, thus I would encourage you to view map reading not just as a necessary means to an end, but as an immensely enjoyable pastime too.

Perhaps the most difficult decision concerns which type (Landranger 1:50,000 or Explorer 1:25,000) to carry with you. The former cannot be beaten for their combination of manageability and detail, although field boundaries are not included; the latter are rather cumbersome (and more expensive) but include quite a lot more features. On balance, for the Mendip region, I would recommend the Landranger series, not least because as well as being so user friendly, all the walks in this book fit onto one sheet (OS 182 Weston-super-Mare). This sheet folds neatly into a size that fits well inside standard map carriers, and can also be easily laid out on a table or floor, enabling you to survey all the walks at once, and to better comprehend the region and its wider context.

Our entitlement to walk across all manner of private land, pastoral as well as uncultivated, is indeed a unique feature of our historical heritage. Such a privilege should never be taken for granted but should lead us all to value our freedoms, do all we can to preserve them for future generations and take care not to inconvenience, still less irritate landowners, who do after all own the land, and have to make a living from it. It's good to remember that with rights come responsibilities, and therefore we should be careful to ensure we have not strayed into areas without legal access, and should go out of our way to show deference and politeness to those working in and preserving the countryside for our benefit. Exchanging a friendly smile and a word or two, closing gates and taking care near livestock is often all that is required to ensure good relations, and should be axiomatic amongst walkers and not onerous in the slightest.

Separately, since the 2000 Countryside Act was passed, access to some uncultivated areas, that do not contain specific rights of way, has improved considerably. For a long time access to much (but certainly not all) uncultivated land was tolerated but not enshrined in law, but now a legal framework supports and protects the rights of those exploring designated open access areas. Much of the western and northern regions of the Mendips now enjoy open access protection, and this, combined with the extensive right of way network and land owned by the National Trust, ensures overall access to the region is excellent. (Open access areas are clearly shaded on latest edition OS Explorer maps but are not identified on Landranger ones.)

Using the guide

I must confess to having an aversion to guide books that manage no more than a paragraph or two by way of introduction, followed by a rather dry series of instructions that fail to excite. While it is vital that instructions are accurate, reliable and useful, surely any guidebook worth its salt should inspire the reader (or at least attempt to do so). This can arguably only be achieved if the guidebook writer first sets the context and then combines accurate instructions with descriptive narrative. This is what I have attempted to do but only you, the reader, can decide if I have succeeded.

The substantial introduction (pages 7-20) attempts to introduce you to the area, enabling you to draw a picture in your mind of what can be expected if you pay a visit. If you already know the area a little (or very well for that matter), I hope that an old flame may be re-kindled, or an existing enthusiasm further encouraged.

As alluded to above, the descriptions of the walks themselves combine precise instructions with descriptive comments in an attempt to arouse interest. Surely it is good to be excited by a writer's love of an area, and to be encouraged to gather up the gear necessary to head for the hills. Walking is a multifaceted, thrilling activity, that offers myriad additional benefits for mind and body. If one can succeed in persuading others to explore a specific region, developing an intimate knowledge of its considerable charms, this must surely be a good thing.

In practical terms each of the walks contain the same introductory comments, enabling you to assess a walk's suitability for your needs and wants and to compare a given walk with any other in the book. Distances are provided but not times as these are an intensely personal affair. Once you have tried out a couple of the walks, you can begin to accurately estimate times for yourself, which is better by far than a guide book writer offering potentially misleading information.

Excepting the suggestion for a longer, linear walk, all start and finish at the same point, enabling you to plan with both ease and independence. Some of the walks are circular, others of an out-and-back nature, but all involve the ascent of some kind of hill, along with astonishing views for at least some (often most) of the time.

The accompanying sketch maps are there to provide a general overview only of the walks, and to help you locate start/finish points, therefore they should be used in conjunction with, and not instead of, the relevant OS map (Explorer or Landranger).

I sincerely hope the book works for you, and that as well as trying out some/all of the walks, you will plot routes of your own. If a fraction of my affection for these hills can be shared and passed on to others, then a worthwhile objective will have been achieved.

Getting to/from the area

It will probably come as no surprise that those with their own vehicle will be best placed to access the Mendips. A number of quite good A-roads encircle the region, including in particular the A38, A368, A371 and A37. But note also that the M5 can serve as an excellent gateway when approaching from the south and west.

For those arriving by train there is only one realistic option, but it is a good one. Trains regularly stop at Weston-super-Mare, a short distance from where the West Mendip Way (referred to throughout as the WMW) begins, providing excellent, on foot access to the western fringes of the hills. Weston Station also serves as a good departure point at the end of a walk or longer stay in the area.

Buses run between Weston, Cheddar and Wells (and between Weston and Brean Down), but for up-to-date details you would be wise to contact one of the tourist information centres (TICs) listed in the guide.

Country Code

It goes without saying that all walkers should be familiar with, and put into practice, the Country Code, and therefore by way of reminder, it is included in full below:

- Guard against all risk of fire
- Fasten all gates
- Keep dogs under control
- Keep to public footpaths across farmland, and avoid taking short cuts which cause erosion
- Use gates and stiles to cross fences, hedges and walls
- Leave livestock, crops and machinery alone
- Take your litter home
- Help to keep all water clean
- Protect wildlife, plants and trees
- Take special care on country roads
- Make no unnecessary noise

A stone seat high on the Mendip Hills, with the inscription:
'Only a hill but all of life to me'

Walk 1: Brean Down

▲ **Start/Finish and Parking**: There is a car park at the end of the narrow road that runs adjacent to the coast and terminates beneath Brean Down (£2.50 for the day, summer 2010). Note that there is another (cheaper) car park a little further on, accessed from the track which continues from where the road terminates. Further, if you subsequently spend money in the adjacent café, matching or exceeding the price of parking, the fee is generously waived.

▲ **Distance**: 5.5 kilometres(km)/3.4 miles(m)

▲ **Walk Summary**: A magnificent walk combining an invigorating but brief ascent onto Brean Down, hypnotic views of land and sea, easy walking and opportunities to extend the outing or blend it with time on the beach.

▲ **Suitable for**: Walkers of every age and type, so long as they can manage the steep (but helpfully stepped) ascent onto the Down and the ascent from the fort on return.

Leave the car park turning L onto a clear track into which the access road merges. When you reach a fork in the track, take the L option between pleasant dwellings to the L and a house-cum-café on the R.

Head straight for the steps that lead directly to the top of the Down, which looks ever more impressive on approach. As you start your ascent, a clear stone pillar informs you that Brean Down is in the care of the National Trust, and an adjacent plaque provides information about the Down.

The 216 steps make for a good workout and are thoughtfully accompanied by small periodic viewing platforms, where the glorious view can be studied at length without hindering the progress of others. When you reach the top of the steps the view in all directions is stunning. Hills, levels, sandy beaches and the sea all compete for

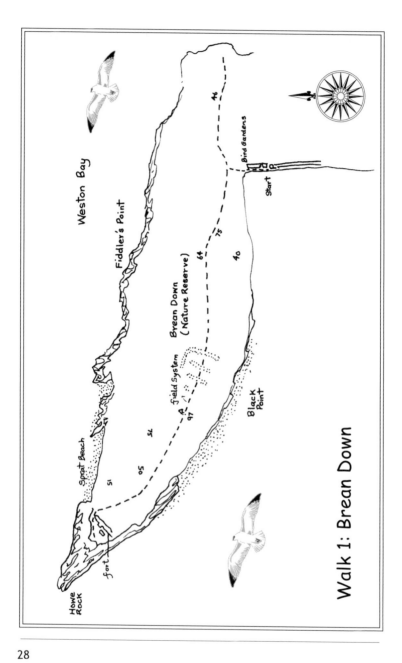

Walk 1: Brean Down

your attention; even Weston looks quite delightful from this angle.

After admiring the view, turn L (west) and follow the crest of the Down to the first rise. From here the view ahead to Brean Down's summit is revealed. The path then looses a little height before climbing gently and easily to the summit.

A trig point confirms your arrival at the highest point on the Down, and here once again, you can enjoy a superb 360 degree view. Despite the excitement of picking out well known hills in both England and Wales, it is the presence of the sea that makes this vantage point so special, along with the island of Steep Holm, some 4 miles distant in the Bristol Channel.

Continue downhill, still following the crest of the Down, in the direction of the fort, which is reached in a few minutes and offers an intriguing diversion. Here, close to the water's edge, it is ideal picnic country, and a grand spot in which to gaze across the water to Steep Holm, perhaps longing for a boat to arrive, to enable the last few square metres of Mendip rock to be explored.

To return, simply retrace your outbound route. There is a low-level track which can be taken if you want an alternative return route, or do not fancy the re-ascent to Brean Down's summit, but it is an inferior option that cannot compete with the thrills of the downland crest.

When you reach the top of the steps consider prolonging your time on the Down by continuing east, and note too that the walk could be turned from a family friendly stroll into something of an epic, by including a stretch along Brean's glorious beach. (If feeling especially energetic on a pleasant, sunny day, you could even start out from Burnham with the Down as your distant objective.)

Here at the western extreme of the Mendips it is hard to imagine a more poignant and accessible walk, so despite the somewhat convoluted access to Brean village, be sure to include it on your itinerary of Mendip outings.

▼

The Maritime Fort of Brean Down

It may come as a surprise to walkers, previously unfamiliar with the area, to discover a remarkably well preserved fort, at the western terminus of Brean Down. This fort, now owned and maintained by the National Trust, was completed sometime between 1870-72 and was designed to deter invaders. The Franco-Austrian war of 1859 had unnerved the Government, who feared Napoleon's aggression might extend to an attempted invasion, thus in 1862 the Bristol Channel defence line was approved. Beside this fort, others were built on both Steep Holm and Flat Holm, as well as Lavernock Point on the Welsh coastline.

In the 1920s the fort was turned into a basic, summer-time-only café, serving tea, bread and butter, and cakes. Despite the basic menu on offer, up to a hundred customers could be accommodated at busy times. However, the café was a short-lived affair; then, during the second world war, the fort was once again manned by soldiers. After the war ended, the future of both the Down and fort appeared uncertain for some time but, by the turn of the century, a successful outcome was achieved whereby the National Trust accepted ownership of both, having received them in a safe and secure state. This arrangement ensures that the fort and Down will remain permanently undeveloped for the benefit of local residents, walkers and sightseers alike.

Steep Holm from Brean Down

▲ **Start/Finish**: Brent Knoll village.

▲ **Parking**: There is space to leave your car in Church Lane, on approach to St Michael's Church (Brent Knoll). Alternatively, there is ample parking space on the main road in the immediate vicinity of the turning into Church Lane.

▲ **Distance**: 2 km/1.25 m

▲ **Walk Summary**: A finer combination of mainly easy walking, easy route finding and spectacular views cannot be had anywhere else in this region, especially if this walk is combined with walk 3.

▲ **Suitable for**: All walkers although a brief, steep section may cause the less fit some discomfort.

Walk along the lane towards the church, but when you reach the edge of the churchyard pass through a black kissing gate onto a well surfaced path, and continue uphill. As the path ascends, it passes behind the church.

When you reach a second black kissing gate, continue uphill on what becomes an open, but continuously surfaced path. Note the seaward views already opening out behind you. Soon you will come to another kissing gate, which on this occasion is a wooden, rather than metal one. Continue ascending, noting that the summit has come into view. A steep, but mercifully brief uphill section, may now test those whose fitness is suspect, but views back to the coast and ahead to the summit, amply compensate for any physical discomfort.

Steps, followed by a stile and then more steps, lead all the way to the top of the hill, where the summit plateau panorama will warm the cockles of your heart.

Allow plenty of time to study the view in all directions, especially

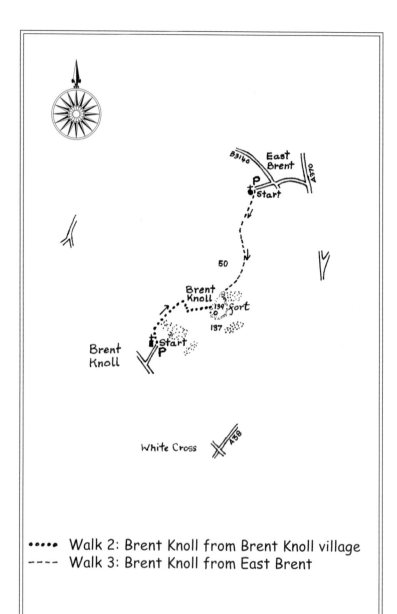

East
Brent
B3140
A370
P
Start

50

N

Brent
Knoll
139 fort
0
137

Start
P
Brent
Knoll

White Cross
A38

••••• Walk 2: Brent Knoll from Brent Knoll village
---- Walk 3: Brent Knoll from East Brent

west to the sea, and to wander at leisure around the edge of the surprisingly large hill-top plateau, before returning via your route of ascent.

To extend the walk, consider completing route 3 in reverse, dropping off the hill to East Brent and then walking the entire route again, in the opposite direction, to return to your starting point.

Brent Knoll on approach from the north

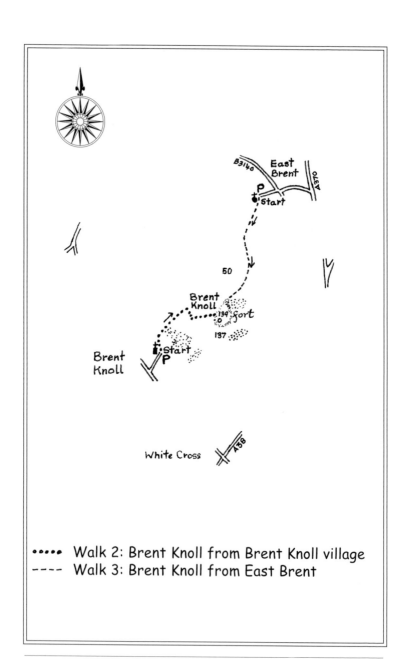

East
Brent

B3140

A370

P
Start

50

Brent
Knoll

134 fort

137

Brent
Knoll

Start
P

White Cross

A38

••••• Walk 2: Brent Knoll from Brent Knoll village
- - - - Walk 3: Brent Knoll from East Brent

Walk 3: Brent Knoll from East Brent

▲ **Start/Finish**: East Brent village.

▲ **Parking**: It is probably best to park (with care and consideration) in Church Lane, which leads to St Mary the Virgin Church and the start of the walk.

▲ **Distance**: 2.25 km/1.4 m

▲ **Walk Summary**: A short but delightful walk to the summit of an exquisite hill, that will reward every ounce of effort many times over.

▲ **Suitable for**: Walkers of all ages although the uphill nature of the walk may render it a little too rigorous for some.

Enter the churchyard of St Mary the Virgin Church and turn L. (Be sure not to miss the opportunity to explore the interior of this splendid church at either the beginning or end of your walk.) Leave the churchyard through a gate leading onto an enclosed path beside a school. Shortly you will reach a kissing gate, after which the path turns at a right angle as Brent Knoll's summit comes into view for the first time. Here, it is hard to imagine a more tranquil and rural spot so close to the M5!

The next gate leads to open country but with trees on the L. Continue to another gate and stile and then head uphill towards the summit. Now a spectacular view begins to open out. When you reach another stile and old gate, continue uphill, shortly passing over yet another stile. Ahead of you is a conspicuous wooden pole, which can be used as a guide to the summit, and which you may well have spotted afar off.

When you reach the wooden pole you will realise that the hill-top summit boasts a very substantial plateau, the edge of which can be followed all the way around, for a full 360 degrees. Needless to say the panorama is constantly breathtaking, and rivals any other in the Mendip region. In particular the westward aspect offers a spectacular view of the sea, which even the high point of Brean Down is hard pressed to compete with.

When you can finally tear yourself away, return by your route of ascent, unless of course, you intend to continue by completing walk 2 in reverse (a thrilling prospect). Further, you could then retrace your steps over the entire walk, back to the summit of Brent Knoll, and thence back down to East Brent and your starting point.

Introduction to the Crook Peak Quartet

It might appear somewhat over-the-top to include four separate ascents of one solitary hill in a small guidebook such as this. However, I believe such a strategy to be appropriate for reasons briefly outlined below.

First, Crook Peak boasts a unique shape and profile amongst all Mendip hills and viewpoints, which includes its eye-catching spurs used as routes of ascent, thus many options present themselves. Second, the routes selected are all sufficiently different (but not in the least bit contrived) to render them suitable for consideration as separate walks. I sincerely hope you agree with this assessment and will go on to enjoy all the routes, along with a fuller appreciation of Crook Peak's diverse appeal. Like a true mountain many times the size, this shapely little hill has many faces, but its classic rocky summit makes it both easily recognisable and highly desirable from almost any angle.

Walk 4: Crook Peak from Loxton

▲ **Start/Finish**: Loxton village.

▲ **Parking**: A few options in the village, but it is important to park with consideration and care.

▲ **Distance**: 5.5 km/3.4 m

▲ **Walk Summary**: Ironically, although Crook Peak reveals many striking features to those viewing it from the west, this is, in the author's view, the least appealing route to the summit. However, Loxton is a lovely village from which to begin an ascent and views of the hill from here are stirring. Further, if one combines this route with one from the east (making Compton Bishop your turning point), it takes on a different dimension and becomes a much more attractive proposition.

▲ **Suitable for**: Hill walking enthusiasts who like to explore a hill from every angle or those who intend to combine routes from both the west and east. Young children will probably find this route rather dull, due to the amount of lane walking involved.

The walk begins in Church Lane in the centre of the village. Walk along the lane (towards Crook Peak) which shortly comes to an end (but note that to the left a concealed path leads to Loxton's 13th Century Church, which is accessed via a wooden archway bearing the inscription 'To the Glory of God'. This church is well worth a visit and enjoys a superb location, tucked quietly away but with excellent views of the Peak). At the end of Church Lane note a stile to your R, cross it and then shortly after cross another to enter a field. Crook Peak now looks a very worthy objective.

Pass through the field on a slightly diagonal bearing to reach in a few moments, a gate and stile. Turn R here onto a lane. When you reach another gate turn L onto a country road pavement, which immediately crosses the motorway (M5). Straight ahead of you is the

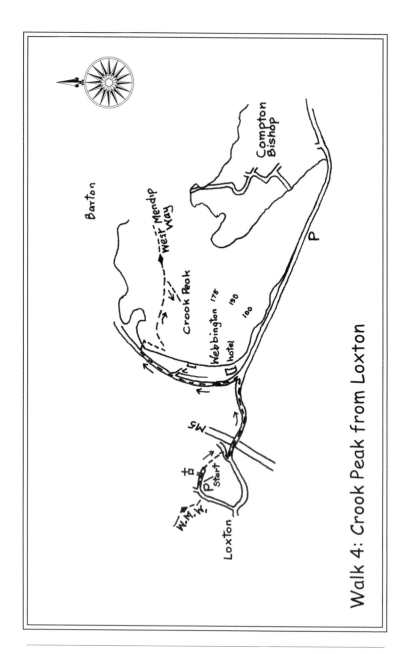

Walk 4: Crook Peak from Loxton

Webbington Hotel, which due largely to an inappropriate extension, represents an unpleasant eyesore.

When the pavement ends follow the road edge for a few moments until you reach a turning to the L, signposted for Winscombe (3 miles). The turning is immediately adjacent to Webbington Farm and you are joining Barton Lane. Continue along the lane which is much quieter than the brief stretch of road you have just utilised. Soon after passing an isolated dwelling - The Paddock - look out for a wooden marker post on the R where you need to turn almost back on yourself, to access the hill via an obvious route through the trees.

Enter the trees via a gate, noting that temporarily you are heading in the opposite direction to that when you were walking along the lane a few moments before. Shortly the path swings L (and uphill) besides another wooden marker post. As you ascend the trees begin to thin out and are replaced by gorse and then open hillside. Continue uphill on the main stony path, ignoring deviant alternative paths that, no doubt, cut some corners but add to the erosion of the hillside.

Glancing to your R Crook Peak's rocky summit is now clearly in view, but stay on the path until you reach another wooden marker post, close to the termination of a typical Mendip dry stone wall. Turn R here and stride out for the summit of the hill, now just a few moments away. As you approach the summit, scattered rocks contribute to the mini-mountain atmosphere, before the final summit clamber provides a fitting finale.

Crook Peak's summit panorama is second to none (save, perhaps, Brent Knoll's) in the entire Mendip region, so allow yourself plenty of time for landscape assessment and personal reflection, before retracing your outbound steps to return to the village of Loxton.

Crook Peak from Loxton

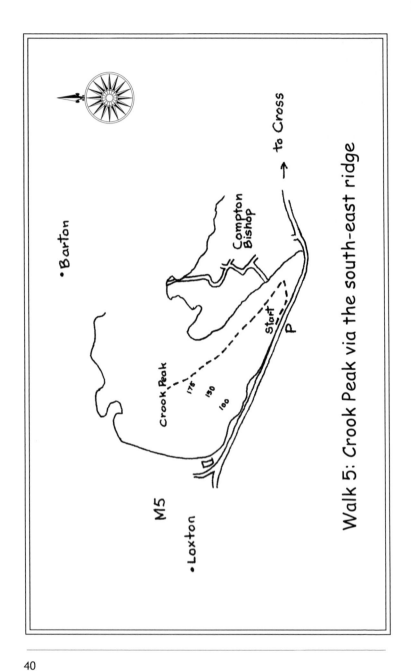

Walk 5: Crook Peak via the south-east ridge

Walk 5: Crook Peak via the south-east ridge

▲ **Start/Finish and Parking**: A roadside car park on the L hand side close to the foot of Crook Peak's south-east ridge, just over half a mile west of the turning for Compton Bishop. The road in question links the villages of Cross and Loxton.

▲ **Distance**: 3 km/1.85 m

▲ **Walk Summary**: A simple ascent to the summit of a wonderful hill and viewpoint, via an exquisite ridge, which offers superb views in all directions.

▲ **Suitable for**: Walkers of all ages and types on account of its brevity and relatively gentle gradient.

To begin the walk, cross the road, and ignoring the gate straight ahead of you, turn R beside a Crook Peak interpretive sign, to follow (via another gate) a concealed path which runs parallel to the road.

When the path reaches the foot of Crook Peak's long, south-eastern spur, turn L, and after passing through a wooden access point, ascend the ridge, heading straight for the summit. Very soon a wonderful, airy view delights the eye, as height is gained and steep slopes drop away to the L and R. Note tiny Compton Bishop (to your R), nestled peacefully in the valley, and encircled by the hills.

Continue your ascent, passing through a gap in a small group of trees and gorse, spying the conspicuous summit ahead. Moments from the summit the ground becomes increasingly rocky, and the hill exudes a distinctly mountainous aura: only in altitude is the lowland classification of this ridge betrayed.

When you reach the summit, a splendid view in all directions will no doubt detain you for some time, and cause you to contemplate whether a longer walk should be considered. But should you have no opportunity to extend the walk on this occasion, descend via your outbound route, again enjoying the extensive panorama (probably superior on descent) every step of the way.

Compton Bishop nestled in the valley and encircled by hills

Loxton and the Bristol Channel coastline from Crook Peak

Walk 6: Crook Peak via Compton Bishop

▲ **Start/Finish and Parking**: A roadside car park on the L hand side close to the foot of Crook Peak's south-east ridge, just over half a mile west of the turning for Compton Bishop. The road in question links the villages of Cross and Loxton. Note: The start-point is identical to that for walk 5.

▲ **Distance**: 3.2 km/2 m

▲ **Walk Summary**: A brief but delightful walk that is rich in contrast and variety, and which climbs a fine hill via a direct yet secretive route. Note too that the walk could easily be combined with an out-and-back extension to either Wavering Down (east), Loxton (west) or for the energetic, both!

▲ **Suitable for**: Walkers of all ages and types on account of its brevity and relatively gentle gradient.

As with walk 5, to begin the walk, cross the road, and ignoring the gate straight ahead of you, turn R beside a Crook Peak interpretive sign, to follow (via another gate) a concealed path which runs parallel to the road. But when you shortly reach the foot of the ridge, instead of turning L to climb it, head straight over it to join a narrow, concealed path that descends amongst trees, in the same direction (north-west) as the ridge. Soon the path forks; take the R option and continue until you are within a couple of metres of a gate. Bear L here to continue on a clear path through the trees. (Note: To visit the quaint village of Compton Bishop pass through the aforementioned gate and turn R onto a lane (Vicarage Lane). When you shortly reach a junction turn L and in a few moments you will arrive beside St. Andrew's Church, a serene spot from which to admire the encircling hills and enjoy a few moments of quiet contemplation. See the inset with walk 7 for more information about the church.)

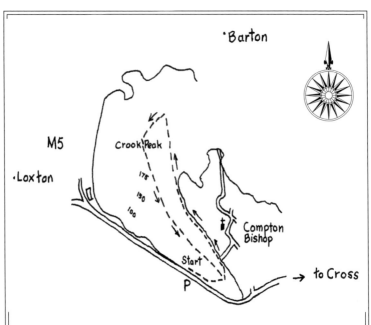

Barton

M5

·Loxton

Crook Peak

175
130
100

Compton
Bishop

Start

P

→ to Cross

Walk 6: Crook Peak via Compton Bishop

Looking east from the summit of Crook Peak

Continue via a wooden passing point and through the trees with a wall to your R. Note the very grand house and grounds below you, the other side of the wall, whilst trying not to envy the occupier. When another choice of paths is offered take the R hand one. This path shortly comes out of the trees but they remain close by on the L, while a hedge is now immediately adjacent to the R. When you reach another wooden passing point, continue straight on but not before looking back at the lovely view of Compton Bishop framed by the high hills.

The route now re-enters the trees and once again a wooden passing point is reached. Beyond, as substantial height is gained, the environs take on an otherworldly feel, the steep hillsides being punctuated by craggy limestone outcrops and copious gorse: this is true upland country.

When you arrive at the summit of the pass, turn L to ascend the ever impressive Crook Peak, there to enjoy a summit panorama of timeless appeal. On the clearest of days the scale and scope of the view is breathtaking and time should be carefully allocated for enjoying it to the full.

When you can eventually tear yourself away, leave the summit to the south-east, heading down the prominent and aesthetically pleasing ridge towards Compton Bishop. The view ahead is now dominated by the Levels, and to the L by the Wavering Down ridge. Soon the ridge narrows and steepens simultaneously, providing an elevated and airy sensation. Note the rich green valley and the contrasting uncultivated hillside - a pleasant combination.

Pass through a gap in a small area of gorse and trees, and continue down the ridge. Sadly this lovely spur ends all too quickly. When you reach a wooden passing point (which you should recognise from the early stages of the walk), turn sharp R, almost back on yourself, to regain the outbound path and return to your starting point.

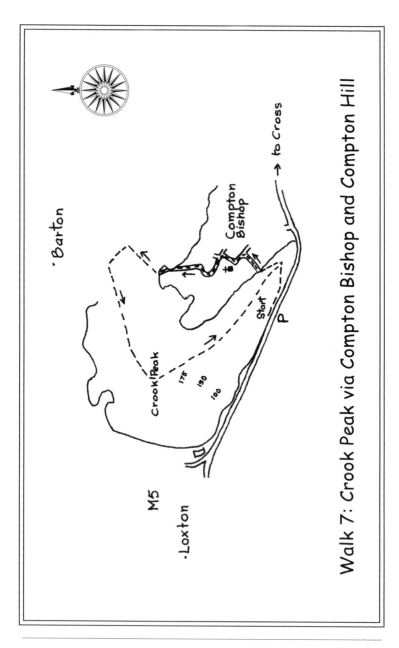

Walk 7: Crook Peak via Compton Bishop and Compton Hill

Walk 7: Crook Peak via Compton Bishop and Compton Hill

▲ **Start/Finish and Parking**: A roadside car park on the L hand side close to the foot of Crook Peak's south-east ridge, just over half a mile west of the turning for Compton Bishop. The road in question links the villages of Cross and Loxton. Note: The start-point is identical to that for walks 5 and 6.

▲ **Distance**: 5.25 km/3.25 m

▲ **Walk Summary**: A slightly longer and more varied ascent of Crook Peak, than the others from the east in the quartet, which explores the adjacent valley before ascending the Mendip plateau.

▲ **Suitable for**: Walkers of all ages and types on account of its brevity and relatively gentle gradient, although, as mentioned above, this route is the longest of those within the quartet with an eastern approach.

As with walks 5 and 6, to begin the walk, cross the road, and, ignoring the gate straight ahead of you, turn R beside a Crook Peak interpretive sign, to follow (via another gate) a concealed path which runs parallel to the road. When the path reaches the foot of the Crook Peak ridge, continue by crossing over the ridge and heading down into the trees towards the tiny village of Compton Bishop.

Soon you will come to a fork in the path; take the R option and proceed to a gate. Pass through the gate, turning R immediately after (there is no alternative option), to continue on a track, which very shortly becomes a lane on the edge of the village. When you reach a T-junction, turn L and head towards St Andrews Church. As you reach the church (which is well worth exploring, both inside and out - see below) turn R into Church Lane and then L into Coombe Lane. Continue along this lane as it twists and turns between dwellings and then heads for the hills.

When you reach a gate (just after Coombe Cottage), continue on what becomes an unsurfaced track, uphill to the ridge, ignoring alternative, minor paths. The path then appears to meander in the wrong direction (east), but do not worry as the ridge is soon reached.

When you reach the ridge turn L and head towards Crook Peak, which looks an enticing prospect, this route being arguably the best way to approach the summit, from the quartet of options on offer in this guidebook. Clamber onto the summit via the rocks that give this hill such a distinctive quality, and then enjoy the spectacular view.

Descend to the south-east (as with walks 5 and 6) turning sharp R where you crossed the ridge at the start of the walk, to rejoin the concealed path, which leads back to the car park and your starting point. (For a more detailed explanation of the descent, see walk 6)

St Andrew's Church, Compton Bishop

This delightful church, which boasts a magnificent setting, undoubtedly adds interest and character to the walk, and thus a brief exploration at least, should not be missed, if at all possible. The noticeboard reads:

> 'Dedicated in 1306, this church has called down the centuries, and still calls today, "Christ died for us." Come in and share the peace of this quiet place; stay a while to pray.'

Then follows a full quotation of Psalm 121 (repeated below using the New International Version of the Bible).

> **Psalm 121**
> I lift up my eyes to the hills
> where does my help come from?
> My help comes from the Lord,
> the maker of heaven and earth.
>
> He will not let your foot slip
> he who watches over you will not slumber;

indeed, he who watches over Israel
will neither slumber nor sleep.

The Lord watches over you
the Lord is your shade at your right hand;
the sun will not harm you by day,
nor the moon by night.

The Lord will keep you from all harm
he will watch over your life:
the Lord will watch over your coming and going
both now and for evermore.

Mendip ponies, grazing on the uncultivated hillside

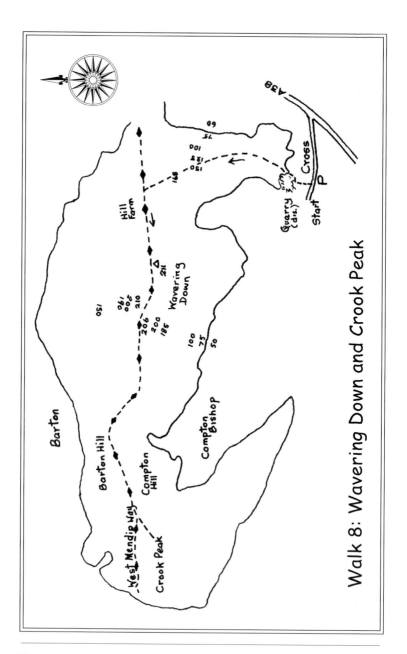

Walk 8: Wavering Down and Crook Peak

Walk 8: Wavering Down and Crook Peak

▲ **Start/Finish**: Cross village, a third of a mile west of the junction with the busy A38, on a path beside Cleevehead House. If you reach a turning signposted for Lower Weare, you have gone too far.

▲ **Parking**: Ample roadside parking including space directly opposite the start of the walk.

▲ **Distance**: 7.85 km/4.85 m

▲ **Walk Summary**: An exhilarating walk offering some of the finest views in the Mendips and including a visit to two significant summits.

▲ **Suitable for**: Energetic children may well enjoy this walk providing they can cope with the sustained ascent at the start, from Cross village to Wavering Down.

Take the narrow, concealed grassy path immediately adjacent to Cleevehead House and walk gently uphill passing through a wooden gate and over a stile soon after. When you reach a second stile and small flight of steps turn R (east) and continue on what is for a few moments, a rather hemmed in path. (Note directly ahead the remains of an old quarry, and be careful when you shortly climb the hill to keep away from a sheer drop to the quarry floor.) Soon the path opens out and before you is a steep and quite craggy hillside.

After drawing breath ascend the hillside directly, or for a slightly less steep option, contour further east first: either way an invigorating climb is a must, and be of good cheer, for superb views compensate for any breathlessness. To the L (west) Wavering Down and Crook Peak draw the attention, but on clear days further west still, Foreland Point, though a substantial distance away on the North Devon coastline, is striking and appears to enclose Bridgwater Bay.

As the hill levels out note how it narrows and becomes a rocky ridge for a while; this is one of the finest access points for the Western Mendips and should not be missed on account of its temporarily steep gradient.

Continue north, north-west, heading for a solitary house (Hill Farm) beside a row of trees. When you reach it turn L and follow a badly worn but narrow path uphill towards Wavering Down. The latter sports a clean, white trig point that can be clearly seen from Cross Plain. At the top of this narrow eroded path turn L to arrive in a few metres at the summit. Unsurprisingly the views are excellent, although inferior to those from Crook Peak, your second hill-top objective to the west.

The path to Wavering Down, shared by walkers and horseriders

Leave Wavering Down to the R (west) as you look out over the Levels and continue along the broad and very easy ridge. Just before the ridge falls to a coll between Wavering Down and Compton Hill, pause to take in the magnificent vista. Although Crook Peak is dominant, other features compete for your attention, not least the northern Mendip slopes where they tumble away towards the sea level valley (and snaking M5). At this point (just where you are beginning to loose height) look out for an inconspicuous stone seat (more easily seen when ascending the hill): inscribed on it are the initials and life-span of one who must have been devoted to these hills for the accompanying comment reads 'Only a hill but all of life to me' (see picture on page 26).

Crook Peak's profile and rocky summit beckon irresistibly as you continue west over smaller Compton Hill and then turn south-west to begin the final ascent. The rocky summit does not yield without a clamber and hides the hill's southern view until the highest point is truly attained. Here the panorama - one that many a fine mountain-top would envy - will probably detain you for some time.

When time has run out, return via your outward route, enjoying all aspects of the walk from a different perspective.

Wavering Down from Cross Plain

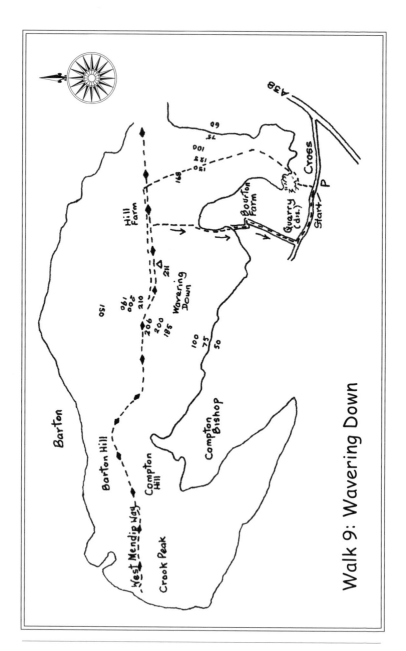

Walk 9: Wavering Down

Walk 9: Wavering Down

▲ **Start/Finish**: Cross village, a third of a mile west of the junction with the busy A38, on a path beside Cleevehead House. If you reach a turning signposted for Lower Weare, you have gone too far. Note: The start-point is identical to that for walk 8.

▲ **Parking**: Ample roadside parking including space directly opposite the start of the walk.

▲ **Distance**: 3.65 km/2.25 m

▲ **Walk Summary**: A short but exhilarating walk, ideal for those who like an energetic ascent and long range views.

▲ **Suitable for**: All walkers, providing they can cope with a continuous (and occasionally steep) ascent. Enthusiastic children may well enjoy the excitement, challenge and brevity of this outing.

▲ **Note**: An alternative return route (mentioned in the walk description below) provides the flexibility to turn this walk into a circular one of sorts.

As with walk 8, begin by taking the narrow, grassy path, via a wooden gate, adjacent to Cleevehead House, and pass over two stiles and up a small flight of steps before turning R (east) to continue on a narrow, uphill path, to the R of a quarry.

When the route begins to open out, with a steep open hillside before you, tackle the hill directly or contour further R (east) for a slightly easier option. Almost immediately, the views are wonderful in every direction, especially to the west, where the dramatic Western Mendips, the Bristol Channel, Exmoor and Brent Knoll are amongst the landscape features competing for your attention.

When the hill levels out and narrows to become an aesthetically pleasing ridge, continue north, north-west, aiming for a solitary house (Hill Farm) besides a row of trees. Once atop the crest of the ridge note the views to your R, where Shute Shelve Hill deserves more than a passing glance.

Cheddar Reservoir and Cross Plain from Wavering Down

When you reach the aforementioned house, turn L and join an uphill path, with a wall to your R; Wavering Down is now only moments away. On reaching the top of the path and the Wavering Down plateau, turn L and head for the summit trig point. There is an excellent view from the trig but to enjoy a contrasting and arguably superior one, descend a short distance to the S (straight ahead in the direction of the Levels), until you reach a feint, cross track. This is a suitably poignant spot from which to note how a series of aesthetic ridge-like spurs add an invaluable quality to the Western Mendips' upland armoury. This spur, along with Crook Peak's south-eastern one, Cross Plain and Shute Shelve Hill where it falls southwards, make up a wonderful quartet of upland vantage points that all walkers will doubtless appreciate.

To continue, it is probably best to retrace your steps to the trig point and thence to the solitary house, at which point a choice needs to be made. Here you can either continue to retrace your outbound route, enjoying the view all the way along the ridge and down the hillside, or head immediately south to join a concealed, almost secretive (but clear) path, between Wavering Down and Cross Plain. If choosing the latter, continue downhill to a gate, which leads out of the trees. Then pass through another gate beside a prominent white house. Almost immediately after, turn R onto a lane, noting the presence of some pleasant country dwellings as you do so. On reaching the main road turn L and head back into Cross village to be reunited with your vehicle, taking particular care initially, as for a short while there is no pavement.

Shute Shelve Hill from Cross Plain

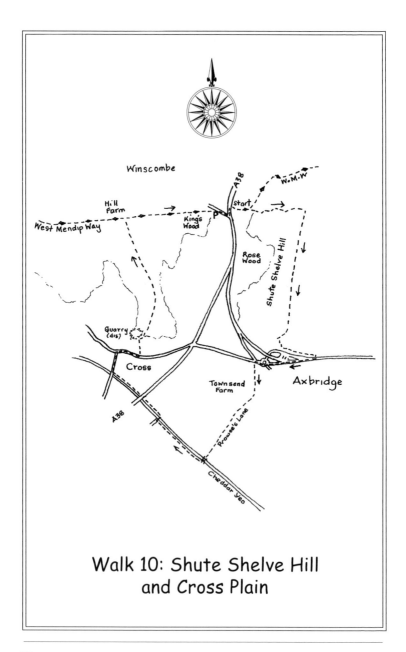

Winscombe

West Mendip Way

Hill Farm

King's Wood

A38

start

W.M.W.

Rose Wood

Shute Shelve Hill

Quarry (dis)

Cross

Townsend Farm

Axbridge

A38

Prowse's Lane

Cheddar Yeo

Walk 10: Shute Shelve Hill and Cross Plain

Walk 10: Shute Shelve Hill and Cross Plain

▲ **Start/Finish and Parking**: King's Wood car park, on the brow of the hill of the A38 about a mile south of Winscombe, and sandwiched between Cross Plain and Shute Shelve Hill.

▲ **Distance**: 8 km/5 m

▲ **Walk Summary**: A quite strenuous walk which includes two steep ascents and one tricky descent to the village of Axbridge. However, outstanding variety over quite a short distance, make this an outing to be savoured.

▲ **Suitable for**: The more adventurous and those who love the challenge of more than one steep climb but not suitable for young children, the less fit and perhaps those very well seasoned in years.

Leave the King's Wood car park to access the busy A38. Turn L and walk just a few metres along the pavement towards the brow of the hill, noting the garage on your L where last minute supplies can be purchased. Just before the garage, cross the road via a useful island and join an obvious uphill track besides a wooden sign, which informs walkers they are on the WMW.

Soon you will come to a three way fork; L leads to Shipham, straight on to a private dwelling (not a right of way) and R to Shute Shelve Hill (you will know you have taken the correct route because you will pass a National Trust Shute Shelve Hill sign). There is yet another option further to the R, but this path – leading to Rose Wood – is clearly a low-level one. Shortly after, when reaching a gate and stile, continue uphill noting how you are leaving the trees behind and entering much more open surroundings.

When you can bear the suspense no longer, turn around to enjoy a spectacular view! From this angle Weston sea front is visible, but Winscombe and Clevedon can also be clearly seen. More immediately

Cross Plain and Wavering Down capture the attention, appearing as one.

As you reach the top of the hill you will come to a gate, but turn R just before you reach it, and keep the wall to your L (you are now heading in a southerly direction). Pass between the gorse and enjoy both the extensive views and mountain-top feeling. Being higher than any other Mendip Hills to the west, in some respects it is a superior vantage point, even if it cannot compete with the aesthetic appeal of either Cross Plain or Crook Peak.

Continue south enjoying a view out over the Levels. As you begin your descent, keep the wall to your L but bear slightly to the R for an easier, though still demanding, route option. Spot the rather uniform and grey outbuildings (Townsend Farm) to the R (west) of Axbridge village, and head in this direction to enjoy a more manageable route (shortly you will pass this farm but first you need to get off the hill safely). Gorse and other vegetation, not to mention steep, uneven slopes, may cause you some concern but persist dear reader, persist!

When you eventually reach the bottom of the hill, turn L and follow a grassy track for a short distance to a gate and stile. After crossing the stile you will be heading south again, between allotments. Turn L at the path junction and continue to a gate and lane (Fennel Lane) running parallel to the road (A371). Just before you reach the end of the lane, look out for, and descend, a flight of steps on your R, leading directly to the A371. Cross the road with care and turn R, to continue along the pavement. In a few moments you will be beside a slip road for road users accessing the A38 south, and adjacent villages (including Axbridge).

After walking downhill along the slip road pavement, you will soon come to a rather unusual roundabout. Cross the road to the L and pass Compton House; Cross Plain is now prominent ahead. The pavement comes to an end but in just a few moments the last village dwelling is passed and at this point you need to turn L into a lane, opposite a sign for the M5 and A38. Very shortly you will pass Townsend Farm (very much in the neat, clean and tidy category) and the outbuildings you may have used as a navigational guide when descending Shute Shelve Hill.

Wavering Down from Cheddar Yeo

Continue along the path which is now dead straight. At this point you have unambiguously entered the Somerset Levels, thus the contrast with what has gone before could hardly be greater. Glancing to the R you will see the Western Mendips laid out in satisfying complexity.

The lane soon becomes green, and blends wonderfully with pleasing scents of farm, sea-salt and rural vegetation. Continue along the lane but look R and behind whenever you can for the views are continuously glorious. When the lane ends, cross a bridge over Cheddar Yeo - a canalised river and drainage ditch - and turn R. Keep to the ditch edge and pass via a gate into a second field.

When you reach the edge of this second field turn R and cross over another bridge, and continue in the same direction but with the ditch now to your L. Shortly you will reach the busy A38. After crossing it with care, continue beside Cheddar Yeo to another road (more of a country lane) which is coincident with a quaint little bridge. Turn R onto the lane, joining a pavement at first, beside houses on the outskirts of Cross village.

Soon you will come to a junction where you turn R and continue once again along a pavement. Now peel your eyes for Cleevehead house on the L - a quite grand magnolia building with glass conservatory. Just after the house, cross the road, and access a concealed, narrow, grassy uphill path, via a wooden gate. Continue uphill and over a stile to another one, and some steps, after which you need to turn R. (Note the remains of a small quarry directly ahead, and take great care when shortly you climb the hill, to avoid a dangerous drop to the quarry bottom, which is level with your current position.)

At first the onward path is narrow but soon opens out with the steep, uncultivated hillside ahead of you. Take several deep breaths and climb the hill directly or continue east a little way for a slightly less steep ascent. As you climb enjoy the sumptuous views, noting especially Wavering Down, Crook Peak and if it is an exceptionally clear day, further to the west, Foreland Point, the most prominent headland of either the Somerset or North Devon coastline, which stands sentinel over this region of the south-west.

The hill soon levels out and temporarily becomes a narrow, rocky ridge of distinction. Simultaneously, to the R views of Shute Shelve Hill - your earlier objective - begin to rival those aforementioned to the L.

Continue north, north-west until due east of a conspicuous, solitary building (Hill Farm) to the R of a row of pleasant trees. Turn R here and head east, with a wall to your L. With Shute Shelve Hill directly in front of you, descend through the trees, being careful not to trip on gnarled old tree roots and rocky outcrops. In a little while the car park from where you began will come into view, and so ends another delightful and varied West Mendip walk.

Walk 11: Fry's Hill

▲ **Start/Finish**: Axbridge village.

▲ **Parking**: Houlgate Way, at the western edge of the village, and easily accessed from the roundabout on the slip road that links the A371 with the A38 south. (As you leave the roundabout and head towards the village, Houlgate Way is on your R).

▲ **Distance**: 4 km/2.5 m

▲ **Walk Summary**: A walk of ceaseless interest and surprising contrasts, that includes a low-level start from a picturesque Mendip village, a challenging ascent, a romp across the Mendip plateau and an easy descent accompanied by spectacular views.

▲ **Suitable for**: All walkers able to cope with a stiff uphill start, but not ideal for the very young and less fit.

Assuming you have parked in Houlgate Way (as recommended above), head uphill to the junction with the road through the village and turn R into West Street. Note immediately, the lovely terraced cottages on either side of the street, and Cheddar Gorge, framing the view through the gap.

Pass beside the neat and tidy Methodist church (on the R hand side) and then soon after, note how West Street merges seamlessly into High Street. But notice also, a small gap (on the L) between the two streets, where a lane (Horn's Lane) heads uphill. Follow this lane and at the top turn R, and then almost immediately L through a gap beside green metal railings that enclose a gas installation. You have now reached the main A371, so take care as you cross it.

Once across the road, note a small flight of steps. Ascend these to join Fennel Lane, and proceed uphill to the R. This lane soon becomes a stony track and levels out to run parallel to (but high above) the road you have just crossed.

Soon, beside a low wall, a stunning view can be enjoyed, in which

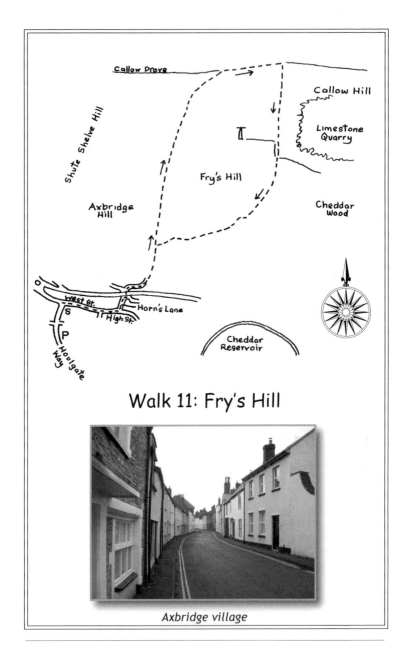

Callow Drove

Callow Hill

Shute Shelve Hill

Limestone Quarry

Fry's Hill

Axbridge Hill

Cheddar Wood

West St.

Horn's Lane

S

High St.

P

Houlgate Way

Cheddar Reservoir

Walk 11: Fry's Hill

Axbridge village

Cheddar Gorge, Cheddar Reservoir, Nyland Hill, Glastonbury Tor and Axbridge village church (directly ahead) are all prominent.

Continue along the track and pass through an old, open gate, noting that the path has become even more rough and rocky. Shortly, when you pass beside another open gate, you will be faced with 3 possible options; following the track to the L and back on itself, passing through a kissing gate straight ahead (the correct option), or over a stile ahead and to the R (through which you will return later).

Continue uphill on what is a quite steep, tree-lined route. As you approach the edge of the woods you will come to a stile on your R; cross it and continue uphill, through and out of the trees. With the trees behind you, continue uphill and directly north. At your convenience, but without too much delay, turnaround to enjoy a magnificent Mendip view, dominated by the reservoir in the foreground.

As you head north, keep the field boundary to your L. Before long you will reach a double stile. Cross it and note how your route has now levelled out - you are on the Mendip plateau. To your R you will see the conspicuous transmission mast, but look L for a stunning view of Weston-super-Mare, the Bristol Channel coastline and South Wales. On a clear day, this view never disappoints!

Cross the brow of the plateau and continue straight on with a wall to your L. When you come to another stile, cross it, but then head in a north-easterly, diagonal direction, rather than straight ahead as previously. As you near the far side of the field, pass through one of several gaps in the boundary wall to join a track, and turn R to continue. When you reach a stile followed immediately by an old-style passing place, turn R after these and pass immediately over another stile beside a gate.

Your ongoing route now proceeds along an enclosed track-cum-path, as you head back towards the Levels and Axbridge. To your L, just beyond the fence, is a limestone quarry - a dramatic contrast to all that has gone before on this walk. Shortly, the path becomes semi-surfaced, and then a fully surfaced lane. Note too, that you again pass the transmission mast at this juncture.

When the lane turns L, continue straight ahead and down into the trees (part of Cheddar Wood Reserve). You are now on a narrow, concealed path, which at times becomes steep and slippery, and to your R is an intriguing, vegetated wall. On reaching a cross wall, turn R and pass over a stone stile built into the wall you have been following. Once over the stile, forsake the ongoing downhill path, in favour of a diagonal one, which initially rises just a little, and then runs at a level gradient through the trees.

Before long the path emerges from the trees onto an uncultivated Mendip hillside, that affords the finest views of the walk so far, in which both the Quantocks and Exmoor are prominent, as well as the foreground features mentioned earlier - the reservoir, Nyland Hill etc.

Head downhill on a well defined and grassy path that trends west (R), noting how the views temporarily become even more comprehensive. The path soon levels out as it takes a more direct westerly bearing, and then becomes more of a track as it once again enters a wooded area.

Ignore periodic branch paths and return in a short while to a stile and the 3-way path option which you reached from the opposite direction, close to the start of the walk. Cross the stile and continue downhill along the track-cum-lane, back down to the flight of steps and main road. Cross the road with care, descend Horn's Lane, turn R and return to your starting point, or turn L to enjoy a browse around the lovely village of Axbridge.

Walk 12: Nyland Hill

▲ **Start/Finish**: Draycott village.

▲ **Parking**: Parking in the village is a sensitive issue, therefore it is vital to do so with courtesy and care. New Road is probably one of the best side-streets in which to park and is located at the northern (Cheddar) end of the village, immediately adjacent to the A371. Alternatively, why not fraternise one of the pubs (the Red Lion is ideally placed – see below), either before or after your walk, and utilise - with permission - the parking facilities attached.

▲ **Distance**: 6.km/3.75 m

▲ **Walk Summary**: A simple but rewarding walk to the summit of a superb little hill, from which the Mendip chain can be admired from west to east.

▲ **Suitable for**: All walkers, due to the easy going terrain and gradient.

Starting out from the memorial to John Card, close to the centre of the village (see walk 14 for more details), walk west for a few moments until you reach the Red Lion pub. Turn L here, into Back Lane, which is signposted to Wedmore. The lane initially snakes to the L then R before straightening.

Shortly the lane curves to the L and becomes Station Road; at this precise point turn R into Milking Lane. Then turn immediately R into Hardmead Lane, opposite Aspen Cottage. Continue along this lane enjoying pleasant views of the Mendip Hills on your R.

When you reach a kissing gate on your L, with a larger gate immediately next to it, pass through it and then through another gate, noting the neat stables on your L. The second gate leads into a narrow field with straight, high fences on either side of the right of way, which prevent horses from straying onto your path. When you soon reach another kissing gate (at the other side of the field), turn R onto a track.

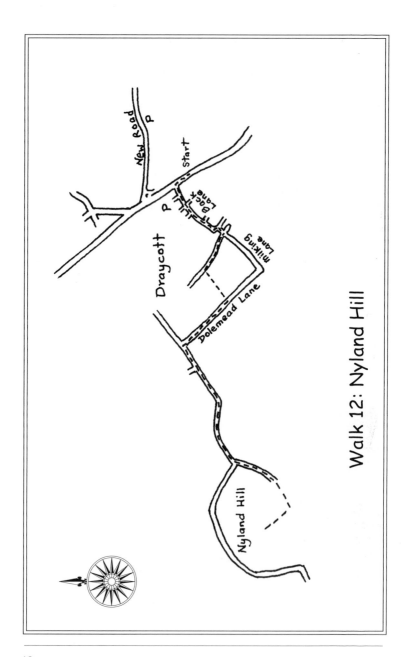

Walk 12: Nyland Hill

After a short while the track emerges from the trees, and, as a result, superb views can once again be enjoyed. When the track reaches a lane turn L, noting that Nyland Hill is now straight ahead of you. Continue along the lane as it first curves to the R and then passes between outbuildings on the R and farm houses on the L. Note that Batts Farm offers 'Quality B&B' and looks especially enticing, not least because of its stunning location.

When you reach a fork in the road, turn L onto a surfaced track-cum-lane, forsaking the larger lane you have been walking along. The track leads past a farmhouse and then through a gate. It then leads uphill, and as it does so, a tremendous view opens up behind you. Pass through another gateway to access the hillside and strike R but to the L of a small wooded area, to summit the hill.

When you have fully absorbed your magnificent surroundings, return to your starting point via the outbound route, or else use your map to select an alternative return option.

Nyland Hill from the Mendips

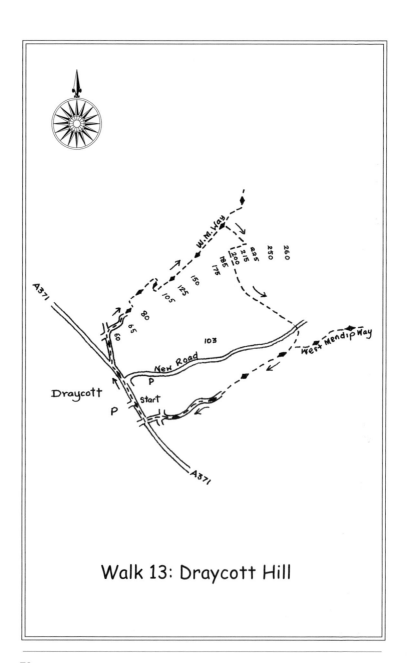

W.M.Way

260

250

225

200

215

185

175

150

125

105

A371

80

65

60

103

New Road

West Mendip Way

Draycott

P

start

P

A371

Walk 13: Draycott Hill

▲ **Start/Finish**: Draycott village.

▲ **Parking**: Parking in the village is a sensitive issue, therefore it is vital to do so with courtesy and care. New Road is probably one of the best side-streets in which to park and is located at the northern (Cheddar) end of the village, immediately adjacent to the A371. Alternatively, why not fraternise one of the pubs (the Red Lion is ideally placed – see below), either before or after your walk, and utilise - with permission - the parking facilities attached.

▲ **Please note**: you could also start this walk well beyond the village boundary, at the point where the route crosses the lane that links the B3135 with the A371, where a small number of curb-side parking options are available. (This start-point is also mentioned with the walk description.)

▲ **Distance**: 3.5 km/2.2 m

▲ **Walk Summary**: A walk which seamlessly blends a pretty village start-point, upland flavoured ascent, uncultivated craggy hillside, breathtaking views and peaceful surroundings (in which farm animals are likely to be your most regular acquaintance). Quite a remarkable combination when considering the brevity of the outing!

▲ **Suitable for**: Energetic walkers of all ages, but the less fit (or those full to the brim after a pub lunch) may struggle with the climb out of the village to the Mendip crags above.

Start in the centre of the village (or, if en-route, from where you parked your car), beside the memorial to John Card (see walk 14 for more details), and head north-west (R with your back to the memorial) along the pavement beside the A371, and pass beside the Red Lion pub. Continue beyond the turning for New Road (one of the best places in the village to park a vehicle), then, as the main road bears L, take a diagonal R (almost straight on in effect) to join a lane. Soon you will pass St Peter's Church and then a school, both of which are to the R.

When you reach a L hand turning into a lane on the edge of the village, turn R opposite the lane, and pass through a gate heading uphill towards conspicuous, craggy Mendip outcrops. For a moment the path is both narrow and walled, but when you reach a large gate the path continues through an open field. On reaching another large gate, continue uphill. Pass farm outbuildings on the L and then cross a stone stile (also on the L), but continue in the same direction (uphill and north-east). When you reach another stile, note the superb U-shaped defile ahead, and then continue over the stile and uphill.

Very shortly, turn R and back on yourself to follow an uphill track-cum-path. This path soon swings back to the L to continue uphill, but now you are looking down into the high valley you were previously ascending. Stay on this feint track to the top of the hill. Overwhelming views from Glastonbury Tor in the east to Steep Holm in the west add both pleasure and excitement whenever you turn to gaze out over the Levels.

When you reach a gate close to where the hill becomes less steep, pass through it and turn R, heading on a right-angled bearing, for an obvious wall. Spot a gate and pass through it to continue to the R of the classic Mendip crags spied from the village lane earlier. Continue east but be careful not to trip as the spectacular vista represents an irresistible distraction. Follow a clear path, which in a while is lined by trees that partially obscure the view. When this row of trees ends, continue on a path-cum-track to arrive, in moments, at a small country lane accessed via a double gate. (This is the alternative start-point mentioned in the summary notes at the start of the walk description.)

Cross the lane and pass through a small gate to the L of a larger one. Bear R and then L with the path, but shortly take a R over a stile and continue downhill. As a navigational aid, small but shapely Nyland Hill should now be directly ahead of you.

When you reach the next stile, proceed downhill but now on a clear track which soon becomes a surfaced lane. This lane leads, without difficulty, down into the pretty village of Draycott and directly to the memorial from where you started the walk.

Nyland Hill and the Levels from the Mendips above Draycott

The Mendip Hills and Somerset Levels – a classic combination

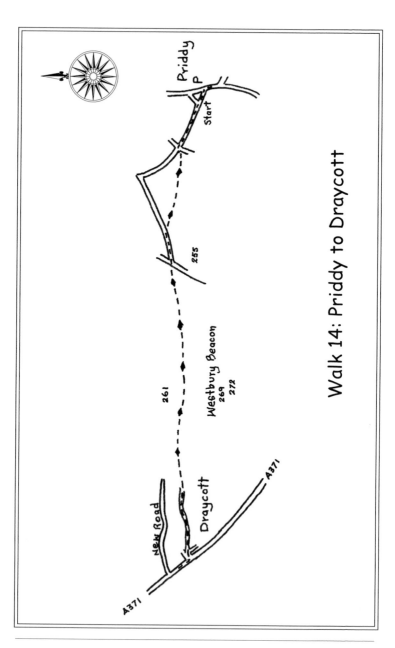

Walk 14: Priddy to Draycott

Walk 14: Priddy to Draycott

▲ **Start/Finish**: Priddy village.

▲ **Parking**: Priddy village centre, in the vicinity of the village green.

▲ **Distance**: 10 km/6.25 m

▲ **Walk Summary**: A contrasting walk which begins on the Mendip plateau beside dry stone walls and quiet country lanes, before dropping down into Draycott via dramatic south facing slopes. Note that your return involves quite a steep ascent back onto the Mendip plateau.

▲ **Suitable for**: Walkers who enjoy an upland environment, rich contrasts between plateau and tumbling slopes, peace and quiet, long-range views and a longer walk.

▲ **Please note**: Stone stiles are very prevalent on this walk, due to the number of dry stone walls crossed, and add an interesting aesthetic quality to one's surroundings. However, they are not easy to spot in the distance, or to cross when encountered.

Begin the walk with the New Inn to your L and the village green straight ahead, and take a L at the immediate fork in the road to follow a lane (the village green is now to your R). Soon the lane climbs to afford extensive Mendip plateau views, in which aesthetically pleasing dry stones walls are prevalent. Then, for a short while the lane is lined with trees. When you reach a R hand turning into another lane, turn L opposite the lane and cross a stile into a field (or stay on the lane ahead if a hard surface is temporarily preferred). Continue adjacent to the lane but on a diagonal bearing that, in effect, cuts off a sizeable corner. Head for two prominent gates either side of a slim row of trees, but forsake these on approach, and drop down to the L to locate your next stile. Cross the stile and continue straight on, noting the rocky outcrops to your L.

The next stile leads onto the lane you were formerly utilising. Turn L here and continue to a minor junction. Cross the road and continue straight on over another stile. You have now entered attractive open country, and you should have a dry stone wall to your immediate L.

When you come to the next stile continue straight on, noting some conspicuous trees ahead of you. When you reach the field edge and these trees, bear R for the next stile and your ongoing route.

Enjoy the immensity of the Mendip plateau hereabouts, before noting a fence to your R, which shortly turns at a right angle. When it does so, continue straight on to another stile that leads you into the centre, not the edge, of the next field. Head in the same continuous direction through the field to the next stile, noting the isolated house and trees, both of which add interest to the scene.

Continue, heading towards the edge of the trees, and shortly look out for the view to your L, which begins to reveal tantalising glimpses of an enormous panorama, which is the Somerset Levels. Note too, the prominence of Glastonbury Tor. When you reach the next stile, continue with the trees to your immediate L. Now prepare yourself for a sensational view. As the ground begins to fall away (very gently at first, but dramatically nevertheless) one can enjoy a unique, almost end-on view of the Mendip chain, all the way to the sea and the island of Steep Holm. Note too, how Brent Knoll and Nyland Hill (the latter in the immediate foreground) rise conspicuously from the Levels.

The path now descends slightly, towards the next stile. Continue in the same direction to yet another stile, just to the R of a row of trees. Your route continues in the same direction, downhill towards Draycott (still hidden from view), with Nyland Hill straight ahead to guide you. To your R, steep, uncultivated and periodically rocky ground provides a poignant upland flavour to this part of the walk. Ahead of you too the route steepens sharply, so take care as you descend.

When you reach the next stile, continue straight on and downhill with trees to your L. Another stile then leads onto a sheltered track which almost immediately becomes a surfaced lane. Stay on the lane, which drops down into the village of Draycott. You will arrive in the village at the junction with the A371 and beside a memorial erected in memory of John Card, donor of The Draycott Charity, who was buried in Cheddar churchyard on May 30, 1729, when the Mendips were a fearsome region, populated by largely poor and uneducated peoples.

A few paces to your R is the Red Lion pub, an ideal location in which to relax and seek refreshment before returning via your outward route.

The Mendip plateau

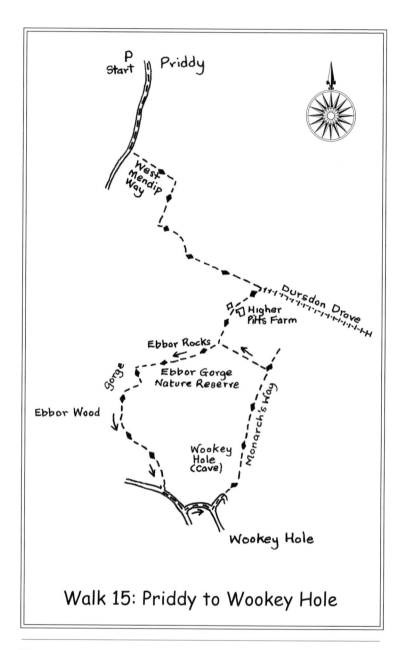

P
Start Priddy

West
Mendip
Way

Dursdon Drove

Higher
Pitts Farm

Ebbor Rocks

Ebbor Gorge
Nature Reserve

Gorge

Monarch's Way

Ebbor Wood

Wookey
Hole
(Cave)

Wookey Hole

Walk 15: Priddy to Wookey Hole

Walk 15: Priddy to Wookey Hole

▲ **Start/Finish**: Priddy village.

▲ **Parking**: Priddy village centre, in the vicinity of the village green, and identical to that for walk 14.

▲ **Distance**: 10 km/6.25 m

▲ **Walk Summary**: A pleasing combination of gentle plateau stroll, dramatic descent (via Ebbor Gorge) and exhilarating re-accent, washed down with stunning views and a brief village visit. Being further to the east than any other in the book, this walk represents an outing of distinction in terms of both character and views, and is therefore not to be missed.

▲ **Suitable for**: Those who like a longer walk, as well as the challenge of a sustained and fairly steep hillside climb.

With your back to the New Inn pub, (situated beside the village green), head R (south) and then immediately branch R (straight on in literal terms) onto a single track road. Pass the Queen Victoria Inn and remain on the lane to exit the village.

A short while after leaving the village, turn L into a field, via a stile waymarked for the WMW and continue, noting the Mendip Mast ahead. When you reach the corner of the field, turn R and keep the wall to your immediate L. You will soon come to another stile; cross this and continue in the same direction.

Now look out for a stone stile on the L, with a WMW and Wookey Hole waymark. Cross the stile and continue in the same direction, on what is now an enclosed path, and follow it as it turns to the L and then leads to another stile. After crossing the stile, turn L onto a track.

In a little while turn R beside a clear WMW waymark, onto a lane leading to Higher Pitts Farm. Follow the well signposted path between farmhouses as the path narrows and briefly becomes enclosed. When you reach a gate turn R, and then pass through another gate into a field (waymarked clearly), continuing with a hedgerow to your immediate R. Glastonbury Tor can now be seen directly ahead and presents an arresting profile.

When you reach the next gate and stile bear R, but pause first to note your position on the edge of the Mendip plateau, and enjoy the unique Mendip view ahead. Here landscapes further to the east can be seen, widening the panorama considerably.

When you shortly reach a gate and stile note that you are entering Ebbor Gorge National Nature Reserve. Continue downhill and over another stile (and gate), and enter a wooded area. When you reach a Natural England sign, warning of a cliff edge ahead, turn L and continue downhill through the trees. (Should you wish to peer down into the gorge, continue past the Natural England sign but exercise great care, especially if with young children, as the cliff edge is only moments away, and is sheer.)

The ongoing path meanders a little, but is helpfully stepped when steep. When it finally reaches the bottom of the gorge, turn L to follow a track. Pass over a stile, noting how your surroundings are opening out, whilst the path - during the winter months and after wet spells - is becoming increasingly boggy. Follow the path all the way down to a lane, and turn L onto it, beside a Wookey Hole village sign.

Pass the entrance for Wookey Hole - an uneasy mix of quaint village setting and purpose-built, commercial visitor attraction - and moments after turn L, into a lane (School Hill) and follow the lane uphill. When you come to a sharp, U-shaped bend, forsake the lane via a gate that accesses the hillside. Now follows a slightly confusing moment: follow the obvious muddy track (to the R) for a short while then leave it and strike uphill to a concealed stile (not the rusty gate, lower down and to the L of the stile). A small Monarch's Way waymark will confirm that you are in the correct spot.

Continue uphill and to another stile, and then to another beyond that, after which the uphill climb steepens considerably. As you climb, keep the wall to your immediate L. After an exacting (but hopefully not exhausting) ascent, you will reach a small gate at the top of the hill and edge of the Mendip plateau. But instead of passing through it, turn L (west) to enjoy an extended view of the Levels, and continue with a wall and trees to your R.

When you reach a stile, continue for a few moments beyond it, then turn R through a gateway. Your surroundings should now be familiar, as you are retracing your outbound route from Higher Pitts farm.

On reaching the farm, follow your outbound route in reverse back between farmhouses, along the access lane and then turn L to rejoin the track, not forgetting to leave it for the field paths to Priddy, the outskirts of which can be seen as you forsake it.

Priddy village and its annual Sheep Fair

Priddy is an intriguing village with a tangible plateau atmosphere, quite in keeping with its location and altitude. Further, it is a settlement of genuine antiquity, with a history dating back well over a thousand years. Beside some lovely dwellings and an exquisite village green, it possesses a reconstructed sheep pen (see picture and quote below), which deserves more than a passing glance.

Attached to the sheep pen (also known as a hurdle) is an interpretive sign which reads as follows: 'These hurdles are a symbolic reconstruction of the original collection which were stored here to form the pens for the Sheep Fair which moved from Wells to Priddy in 1348 at the outbreak of the Black Death.' The fair is now held annually in August, on the Wednesday closest to the original date of 21st.

A reconstructed sheep pen situated on Priddy village green

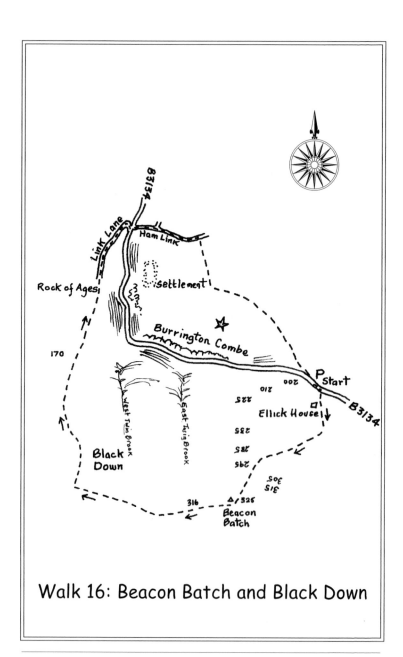

Walk 16: Beacon Batch and Black Down

Walk 16: Beacon Batch and Black Down

▲ **Start/Finish and Parking**: Roadside parking area on the B3134, at the head (and eastern end) of Burrington Combe.

▲ **Distance**: 6 km/3.75 m

▲ **Walk Summary**: A very different walk from those located on the range's southern slopes, and one that offers unique views in an environment not dissimilar to Exmoor.

▲ **Suitable for**: All walkers, although young children may find it a bit too long, and all should be aware of the relatively high and exposed ground to be crossed, which experiences the most severe Mendip weather.

Leave the roadside parking area to the L (south-east), and after crossing the road with care, head uphill past a bus stop. Immediately after the latter, turn R onto a clear path, noting Ellick House on your R. The path soon narrows and continues uphill, via a gate, and out into a classic, uncultivated Mendip setting (the preserve of ponies rather than people). When the path comes to a clear three-way fork, take the middle one, which continues straight on and uphill. Glancing back at this point will already reveal a comprehensive panorama over pastoral Somerset countryside well beyond the Mendip boundary.

Your uphill path soon curves to the R (south-west) and joins a more defined track from the east (L), just moments before the Beacon Batch trig point is reached. At 325m (1066ft) above sea level, this is the highest point in the entire Mendip range, and although it is little more than a swelling of the plateau hereabouts, it is a special place, offering good views and solitude aplenty.

When you have had your fill of the summit panorama, continue west on a remarkably straight path, heading towards a line of trees in the distance, and the Bristol Channel (still further away). Note the red soil beneath your feet (old red sandstone) which makes for pleasant and easy going progress. But note too how the path is almost like a small trench, with the result that the view becomes somewhat obscured.

When a clear fork in the path is reached, take the R option (thankfully, this path possesses no trench-like characteristics). Now the view to the north dominates, which is a blend of Mendip topography in the foreground, and pastoral countryside beyond. Continue on this path, ignoring downhill options to the R, until you reach an obvious and wide cross-track. Turn R here, and continue gently downhill, with the line of trees and Bristol Channel now to your L. (As you descend, note dramatic Burrington Combe ahead and to the R.) Stay on this wide and gentle track downhill and into the trees, continuing over a cross-track a few moments before the trees are reached.

After entering the trees, you will soon come to a T-junction. Turn R here onto a track-cum-lane, and cross a cattle-grid, a short while after which the track becomes surfaced. Follow the lane (Link Lane) to the main road (B3134), which needs to be crossed with care. Directly opposite Link Lane is another, called Ham Link; follow it to continue the walk.

Stay on this lane, passing an 'unsuitable for motors' sign, and between dwellings. The lane soon narrows and steepens. When you reach the brow of the hill, turn R through a gate, into a wooded area and onto a clear uphill path. Continue, ignoring any alternative path options. After a while, a parallel track can be seen immediately to the R, and moments later, this track and your existing path merge. Once again, continue uphill ignoring branch path options.

Shortly the path emerges from the trees out onto the Mendip plateau once more, but this time north of the Burrington Combe gorge. Now you will see the route to Beacon Batch, with which you began the walk.

Stay on the main, wide path, and as you cross the brow of the plateau, Ellick House can be clearly seen, ahead. A gentle descent then leads to a brief, stony path, which accesses the car park from where you commenced the walk.

▼

Burrington Combe

Walks 16 to 18 boast the additional advantage of being immediately adjacent to Burrington Combe, a remarkable gorge which, in some respects, even surpasses its more famous and sheer-sided neighbour, Cheddar Gorge. Whilst Burrington cannot compete with Cheddar's rocky drama and wide range of activities on offer, it too is home to many caves and provides motorists and self-propelled visitors with breathtaking views on all sides. However, unlike Cheddar it is almost completely undeveloped, save the Burrington Inn, a small car park at either end of the gorge and, of course, the road running where once a river did. This undeveloped aspect is particularly endearing, and gives the gorge an added quality which its busier neighbour cannot match.

Ascending the gorge is possible at various points from the roadside, but care and caution is required to ensure a safe route has been selected. Such adventures are beyond the scope of this guidebook but, ironically perhaps, the easiest walk in the book enables all walkers to view the gorge from above and to study its complexity at leisure and in safety.

Dramatic Burrington Combe, viewed from the gentlest of Mendip strolls

Walk 17: Burrington Ham

▲ **Start/Finish and Parking**: Roadside parking area on the B3134, at the head (and eastern end) of Burrington Combe.

▲ **Distance**: 1.5 km/1 m

▲ **Walk Summary**: The simplest of Mendip strolls, but one that offers a setting of real drama, especially when standing above Burrington Combe.

▲ **Suitable for**: All walkers, due to its brevity and easy gradient, but young children should not be left unsupervised near the top of the gorge.

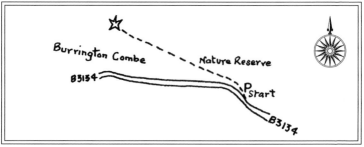

With your back to the road, leave the parking area to the L on a path that climbs gently away from the car park, to access the moorland adjacent to Burrington Combe. A few moments after emerging from the top of the path turn L and continue amidst pleasant surroundings with views of Beacon Batch to your L. After a while the path descends a little before climbing to a rocky, limestone protrusion, from where a delightful 360 degree view can be studied at leisure.

To vary your return and take in a spectacular view of the gorge, follow momentarily your outward route, but when the path forks, take the R option to reach the top of the gorge shortly after. If with small children, take great care here, as the slopes to the gorge bottom are very steep, but don't miss the opportunity to peer down to the road below. Then, with your back to the gorge, spy a clear path to your R and follow it. After a short while it merges with your outward path, which can then be followed back to your starting point.

Walk 18: Limestone Link from Burrington Combe

▲ **Start/Finish and Parking**: Roadside parking area on the B3134, at the north-western end of the gorge, and adjacent to the Burrington Inn.

▲ **Distance**: 7 km/4.35 m

▲ **Walk Summary**: A peaceful, scenic and sometimes secluded walk to a magnificent viewpoint, utilising a section of the Limestone Link long distance path.

▲ **Suitable for**: All walkers, although young children may find it a little too long for their liking.

Leave the car park to the R and pass beside the Burrington Inn before crossing the road with care, to access Link Lane. Follow the lane uphill, noting that after a short while it becomes less well surfaced and more of a track. After passing over a cattle grid, prepare to take a L, out of the trees onto the open moorland. When you reach a clear cross-track with the Mendip plateau ahead and the gorge to your L, turn R and follow the path beside the edge of the trees.

Stay on the main path heading west. Soon your route joins an avenue of trees in pleasing and rather secretive surroundings. When you reach a gate across the path (with Limestone Link (LL) long distance path sign) continue straight on. In a few moments you will come to a fork in the path; take the R option. Shortly after, when you come to a gate on your R, with a notice attached, stating that beyond is private property with no public right of way, turn L (directly opposite) and pass through another gate (with stile) to emerge from the trees. Although the area is open, two clear paths present themselves; take the L hand option (straight on in effect). Now spot another gate straight ahead and uphill. As you approach it, turn to note a glorious view in which Beacon Batch (the highest point in the Mendips) is especially prominent. From this angle, the summit area and surrounding moorland is reminiscent of nearby Exmoor and

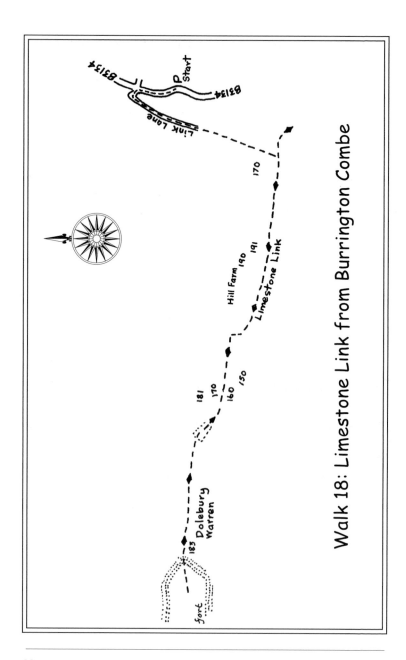

Walk 18: Limestone Link from Burrington Combe

even, to a degree, the foothills of Scotland's Cairngorm Mountains.

Continue beyond the gate (also with stile) noting how both Wavering Down and majestic Crook Peak have come into view ahead. Beyond lies the Bristol Channel, which completes (to perfection) an extensive panorama. When you reach a fork in the path turn R, then moments later turn L beside a waymark post, to enter the trees momentarily. Beyond the trees the view continues to excite and spur you on, and leads to another gate and stile. Continue to the summit of the hill which boasts a fort that acts as a superb belvedere and picnic spot. This is just as well, as it is your turning point, and thus when your time has expired, return via your outward route, or consider extending the walk over Beacon Batch if time and circumstances permit.

Black Down and Beacon Batch from the Limestone Link path

A suggested longer traverse

The well established and popular WMW commences in Wells and threads a meandering 30 mile path over the Mendips to meet the sea at Uphill, a pleasant village south of Weston-super-Mare, that shares the same stretch of beach, but which is otherwise quite different from its rather overbearing neighbour. However, I would like to recommend an alternative traverse that does not meander as much as the WMW and which can, therefore, easily be completed in a single day.

Priddy to Uphill and Weston-super-Mare

If a kind friend can drop you in this little village, it is a wonderful place to begin a day-long traverse of the Mendips. Priddy sits at the heart of the Mendip plateau at approximately 250m (820ft) above sea level. Despite being easily accessed from the fast and straight B3135, it enjoys a seemingly remote location, ideal for stirring one's interest at the start of an exciting expedition.

As progress is made across the plateau towards the steep south-facing slopes, magnificent, wide-ranging views of the Somerset Levels greet the eye, and above the village of Draycott the Mendip chain can be viewed all the way to Brean Down and Steep Holm. When seen for the first time, this view offers an entirely different aspect to those further west, which should not be missed on any account (even if only the briefest of outings can be planned - see walks 13 and 14).

After an extended, high level section, the route drops down into Cheddar. (Note that almost all of the walk has been on the WMW so far, making route finding straightforward.) As you enter Cheddar via the lane from Bradley Cross, the WMW is forsaken but is rejoined later – see below.

Leaving Cheddar via the reservoir perimeter path, you will soon find yourself out in the Somerset Levels, where you can join a path beside Cheddar Yeo. After reaching the village of Cross, a not-to-be-missed ascent back onto the Mendip plateau can be made, via Cross Plain and Wavering Down.

The WMW is once again joined at Hill Farm (just prior to Wavering Down's summit in fact), and can then be followed all the way to Uphill, via Crook Peak, Loxton Hill, Bleadon, and a superb vantage point beside Uphill Castle and the hill-top church of St Nicholas. On this final summit,

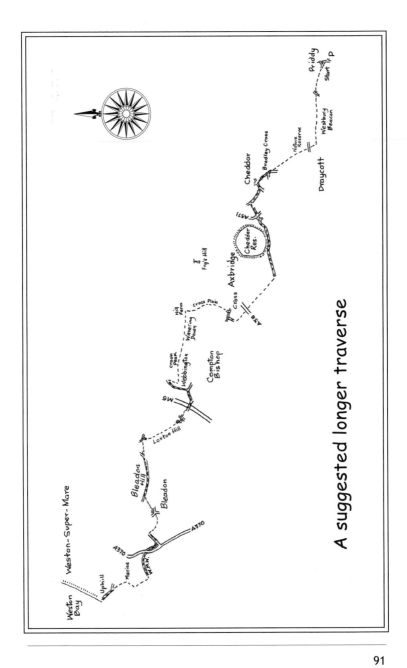

A suggested longer traverse

The Somerset Levels, viewed to perfection from the Mendip plateau

Brean Down from Uphill

Brean Down appears to be within touching distance, but it is the other side of the river Axe, which can only be safely crossed after a substantial detour, thus it is better to appreciate it as a destination belonging to a separate itinerary, however tantalising its close proximity may make it.

A walk along the seafront, from Uphill to Weston-super-Mare, makes for a fitting grand finale, and the town offers excellent transport links along with a wide range of accommodation, providing tired walkers with a variety of options.

This walk is at once both thrilling and perfectly achievable for those of reasonable fitness, thus I warmly recommend it to you as an ideal way to explore a substantial area of these beautiful hills.

Concluding remarks

It probably won't have escaped your notice, that the Mendips occupy a wonderful juxtaposition between steep-sided, rocky mountains-in-miniature on the one hand, and family-friendly hills and plateaux on the other. Coupled with both the close proximity of the sea and the small area covered, they possess unsurpassed aesthetic qualities that other regions throughout the south-west (and beyond) cannot match. With these thoughts in mind, surely no further encouragement should be needed, for you to gather together a few essential items, make suitable plans and go. Whether alone or with family and friends, I can happily assure you that the Mendips will not disappoint, but rather, will provide days of unforgettable pleasure.

Happy walking and exploring.

Tourist Information Centres (TICs)

TICs play a vital role in providing information about attractions, accommodation, public transport and much more. With this in mind, the telephone numbers of those of especial relevance to the Mendip region covered in this book are provided (see below). In particular, if planning to use buses to access the Mendips, these centres will be able to provide you with up-to-date information.

Weston-super-Mare	01934 888800
Cheddar	01934 744071
Wells	01749 672552

Acknowledgements

I would like to thank my sister-in-law, Joan Alsop, for producing the excellent sketch maps for this guidebook. Special thanks also to Roger Jones for his kindness, skill and professionalism when preparing this book for publication. Finally, I wish to thank my youngest daughter, Isabella, for accompanying her daddy on many of the walks, even if she did have to be bribed with the promise of ice creams and shoulder rides!

About the author

James Alsop has been a walking enthusiast for many years, during which time he has climbed more than 150 separate Scottish mountains and several Welsh peaks. However, his interest extends well beyond mountain and upland areas. Born in West Wiltshire, and a resident of the county all his life, he feels especially privileged to be surrounded by a host of delightful walking destinations (both within and beyond the county's borders), including the Pewsey Downs to the east, the Deverills to the south, the Mendips to the west and the Cotswolds to the north, and is often to be found roaming these favourite areas, as well as others a little further afield.

James is an active member of Wiltshire and Swindon Countryside Access Forum and is passionately committed to the preservation of excellent, ongoing relations between landowners, rights of way professionals and outdoor enthusiasts.

James lectures in Tourism, Business and Politics at Wiltshire College. He is married to Kate, and they have two daughters, Evangeline and Isabella.

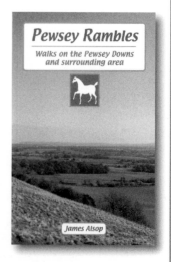